CHERYL SALISBURY · JOHNNY WARREN
· LISA DE VANNA ·
· MILE JEDINAK ·
RY KEWELL · TIM CAHILL · LISA DE V
KERR · MARK SCHWARZER · MILE J
JULIE DOLAN · HARRY KEWELL · TI
MARK VIDUKA · SAM KERR · MARK SC
OHNNY WARREN · JULIE DOLAN · HA
· CRAIG JOHNSTON · MARK VIDUKA
AK · CHERYL SALISBURY · JOHNNY W
HILL · LISA DE VANNA · CRAIG JOHN
WARZER · MILE JEDINAK · CHERYL SA
RRY KEWELL · TIM CAHILL · LISA DE
KERR · MARK SCHWARZER · MILE J
JULIE DOLAN · HARRY KEWELL · TI
MARK VIDUKA · SAM KERR · MARK SC
OHNNY WARREN · JULIE DOLAN · HA
· CRAIG JOHNSTON · MARK VIDUKA
AK · CHERYL SALISBURY · JOHNNY W
HILL · LISA DE VANNA · CRAIG JOHN
WARZER · MILE JEDINAK · CHERYL SA
RRY KEWELL · TIM CAHILL · LISA DE

The
IMMORTALS
of Australian Soccer

Lucas Radbourne

A Gelding Street Press book
An imprint of Rockpool Publishing
PO Box 252, Summer Hill, NSW 2130, Australia

www.geldingstreetpress.com

ISBN: 9781922579355

Published in Australia in 2022 by Rockpool Publishing
Copyright text © Lucas Radbourne 2022
Copyright design © Rockpool Publishing 2022

Design and typesetting by Daniel Poole, Rockpool Publishing
Edited by Lisa Macken
Acquisition editor: Luke West

John Morris/Mpix Photography: pages iv, vi, 3, 10, 13, 16, 20, 26, 27, 28, 29, 30, 31, 80, 89, 105, 106, 108, 110, 112, 113, 114 all, 154, 158, 160, 170, 172, 186, 189, 190, 192

Alamy: pages 4, 12, 25, 32, 36, 50, 82 bottom, 84, 118, 121, 124, 126, 130, 131, 132, 135, 136, 140, 142, 143, 147, 164, 167, 168, 180, 199

Newspix: pages 6, 7, 8, 9, 11, 15, 22, 23, 38, 39, 40, 41, 44, 47, 61, 62, 78, 82 top, 83, 85, 86, 90, 93, 96, 100 both, 102, 103, 104, 117, 129, 138, 144, 145, 148, 149, 151, 156, 157, 159, 163, 174, 178, 182

Paul Jones: pages 42, 43

Ian Collis collection: pages 52 both, 53, 54

National Archives of Australia: pages 57, 58, 176, 184, 185

Nine Publishing/Fairfax Photos: pages 66, 72

Julie Dolan collection: pages 68, 73, 75, 76, 77

Trixie Tagg collection: page 71

Lucas Radbourne: page 200

All rights reserved. No part of this publication may be reproduced, stored in a retrieval system, or transmitted in any form or by any means, electronic, mechanical, photocopying, recording or otherwise, without the prior written permission of the publisher.

A catalogue record for this book is available from the National Library of Australia

Printed and bound in China

10 9 8 7 6 5 4 3 2 1

To/ Rob —
Best wishes & go hard!!!
From Greg Christmas 2022

DEDICATION

For Mum and Dono, with love

Immortal Australian footballers Mark Schwarzer, Tim Cahill and Lucas Neill line up for the Socceroos.

Tim Cahill celebrates scoring for the Socceroos in typical fashion.

CONTENTS

Introduction   1

THE TEAM

1. Mark Schwarzer   4
2. Mile Jedinak   20
3. Cheryl Salisbury   36
4. Johnny Warren   50
5. Julie Dolan   66
6. Harry Kewell   80
7. Tim Cahill   96
8. Lisa De Vanna   110
9. Craig Johnston   124
10. Mark Viduka   140
11. Sam Kerr   154

SUBSTITUTES

12. Lucas Neill, Melissa Barbieri, Joe Marston, Alex Tobin, Heather Garriock, Damian Mori and Peter Wilson   170

COACH

13. Ange Postecoglou   186

Bibliography   194
Acknowledgements   199
About the author   200

The Socceroos celebrate qualifying for the 2014 World Cup in front of 80,000 fans at Stadium Australia.

A packed house at Stadium Australia to watch the Socceroos in action.

INTRODUCTION

Some loathe Australian football as a tale told by an idiot, full of sound and fury, signifying nothing. Scoreless draws and ethnic wars scribbled by hoodlums and zealots, sheilas, wogs and poofters. To others it's just ersatz: Australia is where the world game ends, and not with a bang but with a whimper.

The truth is that football holds an uncomfortable mirror to the society that plays it. It's as boring as the beholder, inviting Australia's patriotic conceit and reflecting its global insignificance. At worst it's an immature culture cringe, but at best it's a pure meritocracy and nothing can connect this lonely, isolated rock to the rest of the world quite like it does.

That's why the following stories transcend sport: each is a unique Bildungsroman. Some of the footballers within these pages were born outsiders longing for a culture they didn't understand, while others were frightened teenagers travelling alone to hostile lands. Some attempted to change a nation, and others tried to connect with a damaged family. Many became global superstars, and a select few scrubbed toilets or posed naked for calendars just to fight for social justice. The remarkable ethnic, sexual, physical and financial diversity of Australia's greatest footballers create the most accurate national representation in Australian sport: they're all united by the round ball's spotlight.

It's been 100 years since the formation of the first Australian national football team. This book is foremost a centennial celebration of the incredible athletic feats – the quintessential underdog tales – that have defined Australian sport to the wider world. However, the individual stories behind the triumphs provide the real inspiration. They're a time traveller's guide from when Australia was regarded as a global backwater whose best and brightest were forced to leave for worldly recognition, a time when professional football meant battling foreigners on their turf for their jobs, and representing Australia deserved barely an inch in the back pages. It spans the length and breadth of Australian football to the modern era, when Australia boasts one of the greatest footballers in the world, yet still the fight continues.

The obstacles each of these footballers overcame reflect Australia's eternal struggle for recognition on the world stage. Thousands of footballers made the pilgrimage; the following 18 are the strongest who survived. If Australian football ever truly finds its feet, then Australia will have found a greater place in the world. That may mean we'll never see the likes of these again – they're immortals because they'll never be replaced.

The term 'immortals' as the basis for this book needs some context and explanation. Borrowed from elsewhere in the sporting world, it's the practice of honouring a very select group of former players regarded as the game's elite. Immortals in a sporting sense are not just high achievers, they are influential identities who set new benchmarks and changed the way their sport is played.

This is the fifth book in Gelding Street Press's Immortals of Australian Sport series. It spans seven decades of Australian football history by analysing and recounting the lives of the most famous and important Australian footballers of all time. It's comprised, in felicitous fashion, of 11 chapters for Australia's dream team, seven for an immortal football bench and then a single chapter for the only coach who could steer such an extraordinarily aggressive formation.

Players were chosen for their impact, skill and legacy. It's the first book in the series that's non-gender specific, and the first to call its sport one name on the cover and another throughout the text. It's soccer for the public, football for the purists and sokkah for the haters. By the end, you'll definitely be one of the last two.

Lucas Radbourne
May 2022

Still in the peak of her career, Sam Kerr is arguably Australia's greatest ever footballer.

With various English Premier League records, Mark Schwarzer epitomises Australia's success at the pinnacle of the global game.

MARK SCHWARZER

Birthdate	6 October 1972
Place of birth	Sydney, New South Wales
Major teams	Australia, Middlesbrough, Fulham
Position	Goalkeeper

Mark Schwarzer was the third-most gifted Australian goalkeeper born in 1972, yet the sheer magnitude of his success is largely unparalleled in Socceroos history.

Footballers strike penalties at 120 kilometres per hour 10 metres from goal, leaving the goalkeeper 500 milliseconds between the ball leaving the boot and passing the goal line. Ninety-nine per cent of goalkeepers guess, relying on statistics, poor shots and dumb luck, but throughout history there have been a select few who can enter the mind of their opposing striker, a psychological deviance that defies reality and allows them to wait until the ball has been struck. It's 16 November 2005, the most famous date in Australian football history, and the entire nation's about to discover they have one of those savants.

Close observers already had an inkling: seconds before Australia's defining penalty shoot-out against Uruguay to qualify for their first World Cup in 32 years, Simon Hill called Mark Schwarzer the 'calmest man on the pitch'. Uruguay stated before the match they had 'a divine right' to be at the World Cup, but they were facing a man who six months earlier had saved a penalty from the striker dubbed 'God'. Amid 85,000 boos and screeching horns there was Schwarzer, flinging the ball in the air, bouncing it like a basketball, tossing it carelessly at Dario Rodriguez. The Uruguayan took a step then paused. Schwarzer remained motionless. Another step, another stutter. Schwarzer's a rock. Rodriguez struck the ball with exceptional power before the Australian's feet left the ground, but Schwarzer was so certain of where the ball would travel that he got both arms behind the shot and swatted it like a fly. Marcelo Zalayeta approached the spot with full momentum but Schwarzer stared him down, treating him like a child and checking his ball lay exactly on the spot. Zalayeta blasted his shot even harder and higher than Rodriguez, swerving into the top right corner, but Schwarzer leapt like a tiger onto a gazelle and slashed the ball with the very tip of his outstretched hand. 'It's as big as we've ever seen in Australia,' Craig Foster cried as Schwarzer spun to his feet, arched his back and roared, echoed by an entire nation. 'Mark Schwarzer, you are a champion.'

Only two goalkeepers have saved more penalties in Premier League history than Schwarzer. First-placed David James saved just three more than the Australian from an additional 14 attempts, but Schwarzer's not only one of the best penalty savers of all time – he's statistically one of the best goalkeepers of all time. He holds the record for the most Premier League appearances of any foreigner, and he has the third most clean sheets in Premier League history despite spending his career with Britain's

Schwarzer saves Rodriguez's penalty with ease to help Australia qualify for their first World Cup in 32 years.

31st and 33rd most successful clubs, making a whopping 836 saves. He led both English minnows to Europa League finals before finally joining a club of his momentous stature at 41 years of age. He then became the oldest Premier League winner and, at 43, the first player to win back-to-back Premier League titles with different clubs.

His international achievements are equally enormous. Schwarzer is the only Socceroo who can lay claim to being one of the best ever in their position. He's the most capped Socceroo of all time and the longest lived figure in Australian football history. He was there from the first glimmer of the golden generation in 1992 all the way to its painful demise in 2013. José Mourinho called him 'amazing', Petr Čech said he 'left a huge mark on the Premier League' but Ange Postecoglou surmised his legacy best, stating he's 'an absolute icon of our game'.

> 'A lot of lows, mostly lows, a lot of kicks in the teeth. What doesn't kill you makes you stronger.'

Schwarzer's remarkable career is made gobsmacking by the fact that he was arguably the third most talented Australian goalkeeper born in 1992. Mark Bosnich is nine months older but had signed for Manchester United while Schwarzer was still playing in

Schwarzer celebrates John Aloisi's winning spot kick that cemented Australia's place at the 2006 World Cup.

Sydney's youth leagues. Zeljko Kalac is two months younger but was a National Soccer League (NSL) starter by the age of 16, had 29 Socceroos caps by the time Schwarzer made his fourth appearance and set a still-standing Australian transfer record when he was 23. Schwarzer's desire was so incredible that it not only exceeded his Australian competition but the entire world's.

Schwarzer's parents migrated to Australia from Germany four years before his birth with 'nothing to lose'. He began playing at six years of age, but as soon as he left the local side his father coached he spent most of his time on the bench. His father Hans recalled to the New South Wales Migration Heritage Centre that 'one particular year, he had a whole year sitting on the bench' but that 'mentally it made him much stronger'. Schwarzer joined Marconi Stallions as a teenager and began taking

Schwarzer saves against Brazil in Australia's second group match in 2006.

Schwarzer and Cahill were the two most successful members of the Socceroos' golden generation.

additional training sessions before earning his first contract in 1990. He barely played a match for the first two years under Marconi goalkeeper Bob Catlin, and when Catlin left for England Marconi replaced him with tough former Socceroos goalkeeper Tony Pezzano, 12 years Schwarzer's senior.

In 1992/93, seven matches into his third NSL season and still warming the bench, it looked as though Schwarzer was destined for mediocrity, but when former Socceroos coach Frank Arok gave Schwarzer his first chance, his performances shook the NSL. He led Marconi from seventh to

Schwarzer takes a goal kick against Paraguay in 2010, keeping a clean sheet against the South Americans.

win a riotous 1993 grand final, keeping a clean sheet while the stands around him were set ablaze. He then won NSL Goalkeeper of the Season despite missing nearly a third of the campaign.

That year, then Socceroos coach Eddie Thomson was keen to test alternatives to Robert Zabica and had already capped Kalac and Bosnich, but the latter Premier League starlet was rarely available. Schwarzer lucked into his Socceroos debut in a 1993 World Cup qualifier against Canada when he was named on the bench, but Zabica was red-carded after 15 minutes. Schwarzer made numerous errors across both play-off legs, but in a stroke of fortune the tie came down to a penalty shoot-out in front of 25,000 Sydney fans. Seconds before the shoot-out an assistant coach advised Schwarzer to stare his opponent down and not commit until the final second. What followed was a mirror image of his defining performance against Uruguay 13 years later: he remained motionless as one Canadian striker stuttered before making a brilliant reaction save. He then infuriated Canada's next striker, insisting he re-place the ball exactly on the penalty spot before saving equally emphatically. Schwarzer's virtuosic display boomed his reputation, and because he had a German passport he left for a contract with Dynamo Dresden.

He landed in East Germany five years after unification as an 'outsider' to his 'suspicious' teammates, later telling Optus Sport 'It was never going to happen.' He moved to FC Kaiserslautern but continued to struggle. 'There was anxiousness,' he said. 'A lot of lows, mostly lows, a lot of kicks in the teeth. What doesn't kill you makes you stronger. It's how much do you want to be a professional footballer? How much do you want to prove your critics wrong?'

Schwarzer's Socceroos fight was just beginning and he only won three caps in seven years after his debut, but his club career exploded after he landed a successful trial with Bradford City in 1996. The English second-tier club paid what they thought was big money – £150,000 – but after 13 matches sold him to Middlesbrough for £2.5 million. Bradford manager Chris Kamara

Schwarzer rose above the rest of Australia's talented goalkeeping stocks, and was the perennial choice against quality opposition.

later told radio network SEN: 'The chairman gave me £15,000 out of his own pocket as a big thank you and said, "There's no way in this world that we would ever have had a goalkeeper of the quality of Mark Schwarzer at this football club."'

Schwarzer's level of mental fortitude was rare, but his ability to read opposing strikers was unique. He joined the Premier League club as a backup keeper, but they were relegated in his first season so he became Bryan Robson's first choice in his second campaign. He made 44 appearances that season and conceded the league's fewest goals to earn immediate promotion. Even more incredibly, he conceded just three goals in seven matches, including a miraculous clean sheet against Liverpool as Middlesbrough made the 1998 League Cup final. Schwarzer was born for the Premier League – he described his debut as being 'like a drug' – and guided Middlesbrough to as high as fourth on their return before they eventually finished ninth. His commanding displays led the club to its highest finish in more than 20 years, and over the next nine seasons he became Middlesbrough's greatest goalkeeper of all time.

Schwarzer playing for Fulham against West Ham in 2012. His success in Europe mirrored his achievements with the national team.

In 2001 Bosnich was in his second spell at Manchester United and Kalac was excelling in the Eredivisie, but Schwarzer's 102 Premier League appearances in just three years had broken new ground for an Australian footballer. That's how much it took for Schwarzer to earn his Socceroos breakthrough at 29 years of age, for the 2001 Confederations Cup. Schwarzer made incredible saves to continuously deny the world's best strikers as Australia shocked

Mexico 2-0, France 1-0 and Brazil 1-0 to finish in third place. His performances were so impressive they essentially relegated the other two best goalkeepers in Australian history to being Schwarzer's understudies for the rest of their careers.

In 2001/02 Middlesbrough conceded less league goals than five of the six clubs above them, which became a regular occurrence, and finished 12th despite scoring the third least amount of goals in the competition. Middlesbrough also kept five successive clean sheets to make the 2002 FA Cup semi-finals. Schwarzer won two penalty shoot-outs within a fortnight against Everton and Tottenham in the 2004 League Cup before shutting out Arsenal in the semi-finals and beating Bolton in the final to guide Middlesbrough to their first major trophy in the club's 128-year history. He won his second – and the last official – trophy of his 26-

Schwarzer continued to be omnipresent for the Socceroos throughout his third consecutive World Cup qualification campaign in 2012.

year professional career that year in the OFC Nations Cup against the Solomon Islands.

The small Teeside club became one of the 2005 UEFA Cup's unlikeliest entrants, but Schwarzer kept five clean sheets in their first six matches to guide the club through qualifying, then the group stage, then the round of 32 before they were finally beaten by Sporting Lisbon.

Throughout 2005 Schwarzer was instrumental in Australia's friendlies and World Cup qualifying campaigns. His November heroics against Uruguay cemented his place in Socceroos history and secured the team's ticket to the nation of his heritage. Meanwhile, despite Middlesbrough often spending little or nothing on transfers, Schwarzer continued to drive the club to new heights. 'Australia is very far,' Cech admired to My Football. 'Schwarzer was going for 20 years to play with the national team, so you can imagine you go all the way, just before the game you played in the Premier League. It's not easy but I think it just shows how committed [he was] to the national team, going back and forth.'

On the final day of the 2004/05 season Middlesbrough faced Manchester City away, the latter being two points behind

'I called him out a few times and it led to me putting in a transfer request and wanting to leave the club. Even after I came back off it, because they wouldn't let me go, he lied to me again.'

Middlesbrough for the league's final European qualification place. In the 89th minute City won a penalty and one of the deadliest strikers of the era, Robbie Fowler – the man English fans humbly called 'God' – stepped up in front of a packed home crowd to take what the commentator termed the 'most vital kick of his career.' As always, Schwarzer strutted towards him and made the icon pick the ball up and move it two inches back onto its mark. Schwarzer waited until the final second, then dived and not only saved but caught the ball in both hands at full stretch. His save broke Middlesbrough records again and qualified the club for the 2006 UEFA Cup.

The Australian didn't concede for the first six matches, then he guided the minnows past Stuttgart, Roma, Basel and Steaua Bucharest

Schwarzer celebrates leading Australia to its fourth World Cup finals in 2014.

– winning two man of the match awards on the way – to make the final against Sevilla. The final was a disaster: two weeks earlier Schwarzer had been elbowed in the face and suffered a fractured cheekbone, and was wearing a protective mask. Sevilla scored twice from rebounded Schwarzer saves and Middlesbrough fell apart. By this point the exhausted Australian had played 350 matches in the preceding nine years, and he had a strained relationship with Middlesbrough manager Steve McClaren. Arsenal was desperate to sign the Australian, but McClaren refused to let him leave. 'He was never honest with me,' Schwarzer told All to Play For. 'I called him out a few times and it led to me putting in a transfer request and wanting to leave the club. Even after I came back off it, because they wouldn't let me go, he lied to me again.'

He entered the Socceroos' historic World Cup campaign just a month later, in the most difficult period of his career. To make matters worse, he was blocked off the ball by a Japanese attacker in their opening match to concede a controversial goal, and Guus Hiddink dropped him for Kalac in their final group match. Hiddink later told Schwarzer: 'I only made a couple of mistakes in my career and one of them was when I replaced [you] for the game against Croatia.' He was promptly reinstated against Italy and shut the eventual World Cup winners out for 92 minutes, only for Lucas Neill to concede a penalty. As always Schwarzer knew where the ball was heading, although this time Francesco Totti's penalty was unsaveable: Schwarzer stretched his entire frame towards the ball but Totti hit the absolute upper edge of the left corner.

The following year Schwarzer was Australia's standout performer at

Schwarzer, in a lap of honour, flanked by fellow Socceroos legends Brett Emerton and Jason Culina.

the 2007 Asian Cup, but when their quarter-final against Japan went to a penalty shoot-out Australia's first two penalties were both saved, meaning not even Schwarzer could rescue the Socceroos. A slightly shocked Schwarzer told *The Age*: 'That's the first penalty shootout I have ever lost in my career.'

After breaking Dennis Bergkamp's record for the longest-serving foreigner at one club, Schwarzer rejected a two-year contract to finally leave Middlesbrough in 2008 after 11 years. He was 35 years of age but still garnered offers from Bayern Munich and Juventus, which he rejected because they couldn't guarantee him a first-team place. England's biggest clubs all had successful goalkeepers at the time but Schwarzer shocked many by joining Fulham, which had just finished 17th, the last place above relegation. He described the team as 'a band of misfits and players written off and a manager written off'. The next season, with Schwarzer playing every minute between the sticks, they conceded 24 less goals, finished seventh and qualified for Europe.

He became the first Australian to receive the Premier League's Player of the Month and won Fulham's Player of the Season. He kept a ridiculous 21 clean sheets in all competitions in 2009/10 and guided an English

When Schwarzer won his 100th Socceroos cap in 2012 he was given a trophy of his save against Zalayeta engraved in glass.

minnow from the qualifying rounds all the way to the Europa League final for the second time. He saved a crucial penalty against Roma, starred in an historic 4-1 win against Juventus and beat Shakhtar Donetsk, Wolfsburg and Hamburg among others to reach the final, a heartbreaking loss against Atletico Madrid due to a 116th-minute winner. Arsenal made three more bids to sign Schwarzer after that final, but Fulham rejected every one.

In the two years leading up to the 2010 World Cup Schwarzer saved three penalties and kept an incredible 15 clean sheets for Australia in 21 appearances, but at the World Cup, for the first time in his career, Australia's giant unravelled. He was at fault for both of the Germans' first two goals in a 4-0 rout and was finally outfoxed by a penalty, when Ghanaian Asamoah Gyan sent him the wrong way in their second match. He even spilled an easy save in the final match against Serbia for a late consolation.

For a moment it seemed time had caught up with the-then 38 year old, but after another formidable season at Fulham – he saved three penalties in the 2010/11 season alone – he led the club to Europe once again, conceding the fourth least goals in the Premier League. He performed incredibly at the 2011 Asian Cup, keeping four clean sheets from five matches, including sensational solo performances against Bahrain and Iraq. In the 2011 Asian Cup final Schwarzer became the most-capped Socceroo of all time in his 88th appearance. He shut out Japan for 109 minutes, but could do nothing to stop the Samurai Blue's eventual winner. When Schwarzer won his 100th Socceroos cap in 2012 he was given a trophy of his save against Zalayeta engraved in glass.

While Schwarzer would play another 20 times for the Socceroos, this was the beginning of the end for the golden generation. Between 2010 and 2013 Mitch Langerak had broken into German giants Borussia Dortmund, Mat Ryan had won an unprecedented 10 Australian individual awards and Adam Federici had recently kept the most clean sheets in the entire English football league. The fact that Schwarzer still played 19 out of 20 Asian Cup and World Cup qualifying matches in this period proves his unparalleled consistency, but also the power of his legacy over Australian football. The saying goes you either die a hero or live long enough to see yourself become the villain, and Schwarzer's 109th and final match for the Socceroos was the worst of his career: a 6-0 thrashing from Brazil that ended most of the golden generation's careers. Critics have argued that Schwarzer was so dominant he shut out an entire generation of Australian goalkeepers, but the fact remains he only broke into the Socceroos at nearly 30 years of age and 12 years later was still playing at football's global pinnacle.

After his 40th birthday Schwarzer said his final career goal was to play in the Champions League, and five months before his Socceroos retirement in 2013 he left Fulham for Chelsea. Expected to be a third choice or even a training keeper at the English giants, he instead made 12 appearances in his debut season, becoming the Champions League's oldest ever debutant at 41 years of age and keeping three clean sheets in his first three Chelsea matches. He became the club's oldest Premier

> **'He's one of the greatest ambassadors to have played the game and a true gentleman on and off the park.'**

League player by four years that season, keeping his 150th Premier League clean sheet in a crucial title match against Liverpool at Anfield.

He capped off the campaign by shutting out Atletico Madrid in Chelsea's Champions League semi-final. The next season he played no matches in Chelsea's title-winning 2015 campaign and left the squad midway, but he received a replica winner's medal at the insistence of José Mourinho. He joined Leicester and played his final eight career matches that season, helping the club narrowly avoid relegation. He finished his career fittingly the next season, winning a second straight Premier League title. Unsurprisingly, he's now a highly regarded Premier League analyst.

'He's one of the greatest ambassadors to have played the game and a true gentleman on and off the park,' Tim Cahill told My Football. 'He's a true professional and nothing but class . . . I take my hat off to him.'

National career		
Years	Appearances	Goals
1993–2013	109	0

Club career			
Years	Team	Appearances	Goals
1990–1994	Marconi Stallions	58	0
1994–1995	Dynamo Dresden	2	0
1995–1996	FC Kaiserslautern	4	0
1996–1997	Bradford City	13	0
1997–2008	Middlesbrough	367	0
2008–2013	Fulham	171	0
2013–2015	Chelsea	4	0
2015–2016	Leicester City	6	0

Honours	
League Cup	2004
Oceania Football Confederation Nations Cup	2004
Europa League runners-up	2006, 2010
Fulham Player of the Year	2009
Football Federation Australia Footballer of the Year	2009, 2010
Order of Australia	2009
Professional Footballers Association Player of the Year	2010
Alex Tobin Medal	2014

Mile Jedinak is the most successful captain in Socceroos history.

MILE JEDINAK

Birthdate	3 August 1984
Place of birth	Camperdown, New South Wales
Major teams	Australia, Sydney United, Central Coast Mariners, Gençlerbirliği, Crystal Palace, Aston Villa
Position	Defensive midfielder, centre back

There's a thin line between global sporting stardom and shovelling bricks. Mile Jedinak is Australia's most successful captain and a reminder that world class footballers are made in every mould.

It was Saturday and a shy, softly spoken 22 year old hidden behind a thick, curly mop of hair was sitting behind a desk speaking to building suppliers. The next day he'd do the same, then from Monday to Friday he'd drive a three and a half hour round trip to Gosford to play another week of unpaid trials and training sessions. It had been five months and he hadn't played a second of professional football. His coaches weren't impressed, and he kept deferring his building diploma. He was beyond exhausted: every muscle ached and he was beginning to miss vital trial matches because he was too physically unwell.

Three thousand days: that's the period of time that separated Mile Jedinak calling Central Coast Mariners boss Lawrie McKinna to tell him he was giving up on football and one of the world's most intimidating midfield commanders screaming at the top of his lungs as he launched the greatest achievement in 92 years of Socceroos history into the Sydney night sky. Jedinak's image, adorned in a blaze of fireworks and confetti, drowned in a green and gold sea of 76,000 fans and surrounded by the bunch of misfits and might-have-beens was Australian football's crowning glory, the greatest triumph the Socceroos have ever had.

Jedinak is the most successful captain in Socceroos history, leading Australia to the 2015 Asian Cup title, the team's only major title. More incredibly, he was the only man in that squad playing regularly in a major league. He's the only Australian man to captain his country to two World Cups. A defensive midfielder, his three World Cup goals are the second most by any Australian and he averaged a goal more than once every four games. He was one of the greatest penalty takers of all time, never missing throughout his entire career. He's the only Australian to win the Asian International Footballer of the Year, and the only one to win FFA Male Footballer of the Year twice. He was named in Asia's all-time greatest World Cup team among a myriad of other personal honours. His career spanned the National Soccer League (NSL) to the state leagues; to failures at minor European clubs to the A-League; to the arduous progression through European stepping stones to the Socceroos; through knock backs and failures to the championship and a starting role for the national team; through years of day in, day out consistency to finally captaining his club in the

Jedinak was one of the A-League's greatest – and most unlikely – success stories at Central Coast Mariners.

greatest league on earth and his country to its greatest achievement.

Jedinak's story is Socceroos history, the perfect illustration of why Australian footballers are different from other athletes. Today, more people know the name Jedinak than Cathy Freeman, Dawn Fraser, Ian Thorpe, Andrew Johns and Gary Ablett combined, but they know it as a passing familiarity. His career was one of immense struggle that wasn't truly recognised by his own fans until it was over, and it will never be truly recognised by mainstream Australia. But that's all part of what makes it so utterly fascinating.

Michael John Jedinak was born in Camperdown in Sydney but his parents' attempt at anglicisation never stuck. His Croatian family didn't speak much English and he was soon playing football for Croatian clubs, so the hypocorism 'Mile' was a much better fit. Perhaps Tony Abbott knew this when he referred

> Most who watched Jedinak play [football] at this age wrote him off instantly.

to the Socceroos as 'Mike and the boys' before the 2018 World Cup, but probably not. He grew up with strong family ties in the heavily working-class suburb of Rooty Hill. He told *The Australian* his struggle wasn't 'extreme', but his parents

Jedinak made his Socceroos debut in 2008 and quickly became an integral member of the national team. He played in the win against Paraguay in 2010.

'worked very hard' and did it 'tough': 'My upbringing was based on working for what you can get. Had I not gone through what I did growing up, then maybe I wouldn't have been able to cope.'

Coming in at 188 centimetres tall, weighing 88 kilograms and with long, powerful legs, Jedinak was talented enough to scrape into NSL club Sydney United as a 17 year old and as the club limped through the dying days of the NSL. He ever-so-slowly developed before the entire league folded in 2004 and Australian football was thrown into chaos. Suddenly every Australian who had a dream of playing professionally scattered across the world in the vain hope of a professional contract. Twenty-year-old Jedinak took a shot in the dark with Croatian club Varteks and died in the dirt after a single appearance. Back home within a few months, he couldn't accept that was it: 12 months ago he had been starting to break through at the highest level Australian football had to offer, but now his future was a TAFE course in building and working for a 'generous' $300 per week for his uncle sourcing supplies and filing invoices. Most who watched Jedinak play football at this age wrote him off instantly.

When he was suggested to Central Coast Mariners coach Lawrie McKinna, McKinna's response was 'Who the fuck's Mile?'

At his best he was a typical Aussie workmanlike midfielder; at his worst he was shy, had his head down and was easily outplayed. But to a precious few there was a diamond hidden among the rough.

Jedinak was at this stage an amateur playing state league football, but after a rough upbringing, a failed spell in Croatia and five seasons with Sydney United he was beginning to emerge from his shell. He had an immense work ethic and a nothing left to lose attitude, and his coaches could see burning desire crackling beneath his studious demeanour. Sydney United won the New South Wales state league in 2006 under Jedinak's leadership, but a year after the A-League was formed the competition for contracts was white hot. When he was suggested to Central Coast Mariners coach Lawrie McKinna, McKinna's response was 'Who the fuck's Mile?'

McKinna wasn't impressed with Jedinak when he trialled, but here

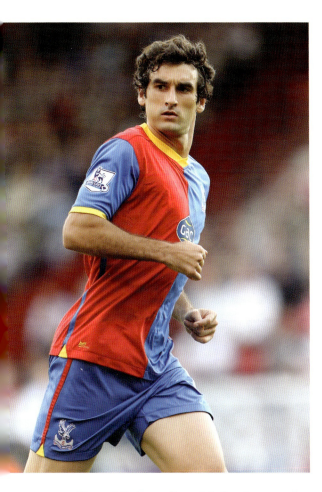

Crystal Palace allowed Jedinak to reach his greatest potential in the English Premier League.

was a powerful young man who was willing to fork out hundreds of dollars in petrol and enough weekly hours for a full-time job just for the chance to train with the Mariners for free. It took five months of training five days per week before exhaustion rendered him too unwell to play a pre-season game in Toowoomba. Frustrated at the thought he'd missed his best chance, he called McKinna soon after and told him he now had to prioritise his career in construction. 'The next day after work in the city, it was 3.30 pm I got a call from Lawrie, who said, "Can you come up tomorrow? You're starting this weekend,"' Jedinak told the website Adelaide Now. 'I almost dropped the phone.'

He was merely an injury replacement, but someone else's misery was the thin line between one of the most iconic careers in Australian football and shovelling bricks. After his first professional match Jedinak thought he'd been outplayed, the Mariners' assistant coach wasn't impressed and the Mariners' chairman thought he was 'rubbish'. McKinna, however, could see the spark: 'You'd think the ball was past him but then his legs would shoot out like Inspector Gadget and somehow we'd be back in possession,' he said in his biography *Political Football*. 'The feedback was great after the game, [and] it also made me realise I had nothing to fear,' Jedinak said. 'I never told anyone, but from that moment I knew Central Coast was going to be a stepping stone.'

Within weeks of his Mariners debut he was offered a full-time contract and everything changed: no more office work, no more three-hour commutes. He had a full pre-

Jedinak stars against Costa Rica in 2013, a match that ushered in a new-look Socceroos team.

season as a salaried professional, and in his first A-League campaign in 2007/08 suddenly Jedinak was one of Australia's best midfielders. He was even more dedicated – once turning up to training after a car crash – and his leadership was immense. He was a steady guiding hand who flew beneath the radar until he'd rocket a shot from 30 metres and explode the raw power beneath his scraggly appearance. His tackling was sensational and his work ethic peerless, but it was that shot, in penalties, free kicks and bombs from distance, that burst Jedinak into the national consciousness. He won the Mariners Medal and the A-League Premiership in a stunning debut season. 'Mile was the key to it all,' McKinna said. 'He'd become the glue that held the team together. Everything was built around him . . . The hair rises on the back of my neck just thinking about what that boy's achieved.'

In the Mariners' next campaign Jedinak scored six beautiful goals in their first 15 games before European clubs came knocking. He signed for Turkish club Gençlerbirliği midway through the season, but his dominance was so obvious he was still named in the PFA's A-League Team of the Season and the Mariners fell off a cliff without him. He also earned his Socceroos debut under notorious A-League sceptic Pim Verbeek, who appreciated the fighting spirit Jedinak's Mariners embodied amid little else. He joined the Ankara club right before their manager was sacked, but hung on in Turkey when most others would have slumped back to the A-League.

This was a watershed moment in Jedinak's career: he represented the first generation of Australian footballers to emerge from the A-League. It's telling that he's the only A-League graduate to garner immortal status, after 16 years of Australia's first fully

> It's telling that he's the only A-League graduate to garner immortal status, after 16 years of Australia's first fully professional mainstream competition.

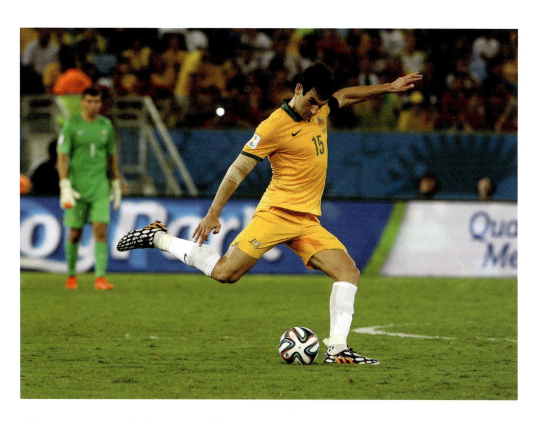

Jedinak strikes the ball against Chile in the opening match of Australia's 2014 World Cup campaign.

professional mainstream competition. That's because while the talents of the majority of his Socceroos counterparts were instantly recognised, they couldn't endure the hardships of European football in ruthless leagues under unsympathetic coaches, and they used the A-League as a safety net that recycled them and mired world-class talent in comfortable mediocrity. Jedinak was different: he fought through a loan to Turkish minnow Antalyaspor to work his way back into the team at Gençlerbirliği and become one of the Turkish top-flight's most consistent midfielders in 2009/10. He also endured a difficult introduction to life with the Socceroos, where he battled the golden generation for one of the team's most vital and hotly contested positions.

He excelled in difficult circumstances: Verbeek would expect him to marshall a thrown-together Socceroos 'B' team against Ghana

> 'Jedi', a sobriquet both eponymous and mentally apt, was a tour de force against Asian opposition.

Jedinak holds the 2015 Asian Cup aloft after leading the Socceroos to their first major trophy.

Jedinak was a tall, bulky, hirsute and resolute physical force in Australia's midfield.

in a friendly, start him among the golden generation against Oman in a crucial World Cup qualifier and then bring him off the bench to secure a match against the Netherlands. His brilliant consistency saw him become a surprise Socceroos stalwart in 2010, winning 10 caps and earning a ticket to the 2010 World Cup to cap off an incredible three-year rise.

He came off the bench and successfully stemmed the bleeding, albeit far too late, against Germany in the Socceroos' opening 4-0 thrashing. He didn't play again that tournament, but when Verbeek left the Socceroos Jedinak instantly became a mainstay, playing the next 13 matches straight and earning a whopping 15 Socceroos caps in 2011 alone.

Jedinak's phenomenal breakthrough stemmed from playing every minute of every match as the Socceroos made their first major tournament final at the 2011 Asian Cup. 'Jedi', a sobriquet both eponymous and mentally apt, was a tour de force against Asian opposition: he was more powerful than his predecessors Jason Culina, Carl Valeri and Vince Grella and promptly scored his debut Socceroos goal with a header to secure a crucial draw against South

Jedinak, who never missed a penalty for Australia, calmly dispatches a hat-trick against Honduras to qualify the Socceroos for the 2018 World Cup.

Korea. His second Australia goal was incredible, a bouncing half-volley from 30 metres out to win against Bahrain. He was the heart of the Socceroos' evolution under Holger Osieck, and he came within an inch of lifting the Asian Cup that year. He made 44 Socceroos appearances between 2010 and 2014, going from being worthless to irreplaceable.

The year 2011 was also his breakthrough year in Europe. He turned down Rangers to sign for struggling championship side Crystal Palace, which survived by a thread in his opening campaign but allowed Jedinak the time to establish his gutsy, languid style in England and build on the confidence he'd acquired at international level. Now 28 years of age, his second English season transformed him from a solid and dependable midfielder into an outright star. He was named Crystal Palace's captain and played 46 matches – scoring a thumping 89th minute winner on the final day of the season – to secure Palace a fifth place finish and championship play-off berth. He then marshalled an incredible defensive play-off series in which the Eagles kept three successive clean sheets to win promotion to the Premier League.

Jedinak arrived at a Palace side that finished 17th in the championship, and after two seasons he was captaining the club in the Premier League. His tremendous exploits and incredible goals made him one of the club's all-time fan favourites, and he was named Crystal Palace's Player of the Season in 2013. He impressively transitioned his physicality to the Premier League and finished his first top-flight season just 45 minutes short of playing every minute of every match. Tony Pulis's catenaccio tactics helped Jedinak evolve into a world-class destroyer who sat in a holding role, disrupted and intercepted

He was named Asian International Footballer of the Year, and when Ange Postecoglou took over as Socceroos coach Jedinak took over as captain.

Jedinak celebrates one of the greatest individual performances of all time by a Socceroo against Honduras in 2017.

then quickly distributed to creative midfielders. He was so tremendously efficient that in October 2014 statistical compilers Opta and Oulala named him the best midfielder in Europe. He averaged the most interceptions per game and third most tackles per game of any Premier League player that season. In one particularly notable encounter he destroyed Steven Gerrard in a midfield battle before scoring a 25 metre top corner free kick in a 3-1 win against Liverpool, which was later named Palace's goal of the season. He was named Asian International Footballer of the Year, and when Ange Postecoglou took over as Socceroos coach Jedinak took over as captain.

His performances at the 2014 World Cup enshrined him as one of the Socceroos' best of the decade; his coolly dispatched penalty against the Netherlands encapsulated the most delirious match of the tournament. It was a hard campaign that formed the bedrock for Australia's greatest accomplishment the following year. Australia hosted the men's Asian Cup for the first time in 2015, with the extent of Postecoglou's rejuvenation stark: Jedinak was one of only three survivors from 2011.

Jedinak celebrates leading Aston Villa back into the Premier League at Wembley Stadium in 2019.

He scored from the spot as Australia slammed Kuwait 4-1 to open their tournament in style but suffered an ankle injury that derailed Australia, and the Socceroos lost their third match to South Korea without him. He crucially returned for the quarter-finals and played every second for the rest of the tournament as Australia didn't concede for 270 minutes straight. He set the tone from the outset in the cup's final, almost scoring a

> **He validated an entire team on the world stage and was the defensive foundation beneath Postecoglou's attacking philosophy, enabling his coach to change Australian football.**

delightful free kick and preventing Australia from losing momentum after South Korea's late equaliser. His unparalleled defensive stamina, despite his injury, eventually ground the Koreans into submission. His ability to lead a makeshift, inexperienced side to Asia's pinnacle is the most impressive achievement by a Socceroos captain.

At the 2007 Asian Cup, when Australia lost in the quarter-finals, the Socceroos' starting 11 had seven Premier League and two Serie A starters, and Culina at Dutch giants PSV Eindhoven. In 2015 Jedinak was the only player starting for a club in Europe's top five leagues. Six players in that final were aged 23 years or under and seven of his team played in the A-League. The Asian Cup's most valuable player – Massimo Luongo – was playing in England's third tier. Jedinak's importance to organising and motivating Australia between 2014 and 2018 is impossible to overstate: he wasn't just the Socceroos' defensive talisman but was one of their most reliable attacking assets. He scored 14 goals across that four-year period and five goals in nine Socceroos caps in 2015 alone. He validated an entire team on the world stage and was the defensive foundation beneath Postecoglou's attacking philosophy, enabling his coach to change Australian football. Put simply, without Jedinak none of it would have been possible.

He came within an inch of securing the perfect Crystal Palace farewell, captaining the Eagles all the way to the 2016 FA Cup final, where they took the lead against Manchester United with 12 minutes remaining but couldn't hold on in extra time. He was cruelly ruled out of Australia's 2017 Confederations Cup campaign and the majority of Australia's 2018 World Cup qualifiers with a groin injury. Australia was a defensive mess without him, limping to an inter-confederation play-off against Honduras. However, his return to the Socceroos at that last-gasp qualifier in Sydney provided his greatest international performance.

His Australian side had travelled to 22 countries and across 250,000 kilometres in 884 days to qualify for the 2018 World Cup, all of which are records. Ultimately, only Jedinak's inspirational leadership could see them through. He scored a hat-trick from defensive midfield – a free kick and two penalties – in front of 86,000 Sydney fans. 'I spoke to Mile about six weeks ago and I told him the importance of having someone like him,' Tim Cahill said after the match. 'Tonight, he was a warrior, he was courageous and that's the reward he gets for putting his body on the line. I couldn't be prouder of him.'

Jedinak was 33 years of age by the time he left Crystal Palace for championship side Aston Villa, bidding farewell to a club he'd changed instrumentally in five seasons. He had a similar effect at Villa Park, restoring faith in a club that had been brutally relegated with just three wins the previous season and were trashed by the media for having a dismal culture. He steadied and then guided the club back into the promotion play-offs in his second campaign, scoring the winner in their semi-final against Middlesbrough only for Villa to lose the final. The following season Jedinak finished his club career in perfect

> 'The other two I focused on myself. This was for my kids to see; that this can be achieved regardless of what others tell you. Stuff like this can happen.'

fashion, a mirror of how he'd broken through seven years previously. Once again his club was promoted to the Premier League from fifth position, and Jedinak was introduced deep into extra time in their semi-final to score in their penalty shoot-out: his 17th consecutive successful penalty. He's now one of Aston Villa's coaching staff, guiding the club's next generation.

Jedinak's unnecessary but stomping exclamation mark on an already phenomenal career was leading Australia in the 2018 World Cup, scoring Australia's only goals of the tournament against France and Denmark. He retired at age 34 as both a Socceroos immortal and a standout performer on the world's greatest stage. 'That World Cup, for me, was for my family,' he told Optus Sport. 'The other two I focused on myself. This was for my kids to see; that this can be achieved regardless of what others tell you. Stuff like this can happen.'

National career		
Years	Appearances	Goals
2008–2018	79	20

Club career			
Years	Team	Appearances	Goals
2001–2006	Sydney United	82	12
2006–2009	Central Coast Mariners	51	8
2009–2011	Gençlerbirliği	41	5
2011–2016	Crystal Palace	178	10
2017–2019	Aston Villa	80	2

Honours	
New South Wales Premier League	2006
A-League Premiership	2007
Mariners Medal	2008
Professional Footballers Association A-League Team of the Season	2009
Crystal Palace Player of the Year	2013
Football Federation Australia Male Footballer of the Year	2013, 2014
Asian International Footballer of the Year	2014
Professional Footballers Association Footballer of the Year	2014
Asian Cup	2015
FA Cup runner-up	2016
Asian Football Confederation All-Time World Cup XI	2020

Cheryl Salisbury, pictured here at the 2000 Sydney Olympics, was the guiding force that turned the Matildas into a world-beating team.

CHERYL SALISBURY

Birthdate	8 March 1974
Place of birth	Newcastle, New South Wales
Major teams	Australia, Newcastle Jets, New York Power
Position	Centre back, midfielder

Cheryl Salisbury is the matriarch of the Australian game. The fierce leadership of Australia's most-capped footballer left an incalculable aura over her national team.

'It all seemed to happen in slow motion,' Salisbury said. Stifling humidity and 29,000 high-pitched screams fill Chengdu stadium. As the clock ticked into the 93rd minute of sweat-drenching, back-breaking action, football truly did take place in slow motion. The Matildas' brains were reacting in real time, but their legs were melding like putty and every stud in every blade of glass was another torturous assault on shin splints brimming with lactic acid and quadriceps bursting through their thighs. In times like this only the strongest survive.

Salisbury is 180 centimetres of rock-hard muscle built on suburban parks against boys when no girl's leagues existed. Her towering physique makes opponents weak at the knees: she has a jaw chiselled from stone, shoulders cast in bronze and the steely brow of a war-weary general. Four Canadians surrounded her, but Salisbury's 138 caps guided her first to the loose ball. She reversed her shot, scattering her opponents, and instantly knew she'd sent Australia to the World Cup quarter-finals for the first time. With one finger raised in the air she strode across the pitch in celebration, catching leaping teammates effortlessly into her arms.

'Obviously the goal against Canada that got us through to the quarter-final at the World Cup was the biggest thing that's ever happened in women's football here,' Salisbury told *The Age*. 'It took a great leader, a captain, a friend, it took Cheryl to bring that spark of belief,' Lisa De Vanna told My Football. 'Time was ticking, she turned to me with passion in her eyes and told me not to give up and that we must fight every last minute. That game changed women's football in Australia.'

To this day Salisbury remains the most capped Australian footballer of all time of any code. Her 151 official Australian caps may never be overtaken, let alone her 171 total Matildas appearances. A central defender for most of her career, she still averaged a goal every four matches. She scored on her Matildas debut in 1994 in front of a few parked cars on a 'backyard field in Brisbane', and scored in her final Matildas match 15 years later in front of a standing ovation at Parramatta Stadium. She was one of the world's most dominant female footballers of her era, and was named in FIFA's Women's World XI twice. She won

Cheryl Salisbury trains before the 2000 Sydney Olympics, which proved a catalyst for the Matildas' modern era.

Salisbury showed against USA in the lead-up to the 2000 Olympics that she could assert herself against the best in women's football.

three OFC Nations Cups, led the Matildas to their first four official World Cups and captained Australia to its first major international final at the 2006 Asian Cup. She was the first Matilda to score at an Olympic Games in front of a capacity Sydney crowd, then she captained the side to a quarter-final at Athens in 2004.

To this day Salisbury's the only female footballer in the Sport Australia Hall of Fame and the only one to win the Alex Tobin medal, yet she retired with no job offers, no savings and no superannuation. In her 40s she raised a son on her own while working as a veterinary nurse to put herself through university for the first time. Now a Newcastle podiatrist, sometimes she thinks she should have retired earlier rather than enter society at middle age and living week to week. However, her sacrifice and determination established Australia's most-loved national team.

Salisbury was born a 'hyperactive kid' to an athletic Newcastle family deep within rugby league heartland. She was always far stronger than other girls and felt oppressed when the only organised female sport was netball, so she began playing football at six years of age for the local boy's team, Lambton Jaffas. She had no idea other girls played football until she was a teenager, but it barely mattered. With short hair and broad shoulders, Salisbury was taller and stronger than most of the boys in her team and won multiple best and fairest awards. By the age of 13 league officials tried to prevent her playing with boys, but her club fought for her right to remain. By the age of 16 she was playing with senior men's teams, so when she discovered senior women's football it was already far below her level.

The only role model she had any connection with was fellow Novocastrian Craig Johnston, who her mum watched playing for Liverpool on TV. Discrimination made her incredibly determined to improve, and she demanded to take penalties and free kicks for the boys and would only train and play with her weaker left foot, telling the ABC: 'Every day at training I wanted to be better than the guy opposite me.'

Salisbury became involved with the Female Socceroos – as they were then known – in her mid-teens but the self-funded team didn't play between 1991 and 1994, then the International Olympic Committee named female football as a new

Salisbury's first Olympic match against Germany was a baptism of fire.

Olympic sport and the Australian women's national team went from receiving nothing to receiving $1 million per year from the Australian Institute of Sport (AIS). In their first match in three years 20-year-old Salisbury was one of the first names on the team sheet. The players themselves were unpaid and completely separate from

> . . . she was suddenly one of the most important players in a national team that four years prior she'd never heard of.

Soccer Australia – they even wore red AIS shirts in their first qualifiers rather than green and gold – but the team had hired a Scottish former professional footballer, Tom Sermanni, to professionalise their passion. He knew everything would begin to change if they qualified for their first World Cup, and Salisbury was going to be the catalyst. In her first 12 months Sermanni told her that she was going to be the future Matildas captain.

Salisbury's influence was immediate and dramatic: she scored three times, including in the final, to finish as equal top scorer as Australia won their first official trophy, the 1994 OFC Nations Cup, to qualify for their first World Cup. The Female Socceroos were renamed the Matildas, and she was suddenly one of the most important players in a national team that four years prior she'd never heard of. The Matildas toured the world in preparation for the World Cup, playing nearly as many matches in 1995 as they had in the previous six years. Salisbury played nearly every minute of every match, featuring in almost every position. The Matildas showed remarkable potential in the Americas, Salisbury scoring in a 7-0 thumping of Argentina and a 3-0

By 2006 Salisbury had turned the Matildas into major contenders, destroying Mexico in three straight friendlies.

win against Canada and starring in a 3-2 win against Brazil, but Australia drew three of the world's top five sides in the World Cup and lost all three. Salisbury started Australia's first two matches and the world stage caught its first glimpse of her trademark ferocity. She received yellow cards in both, suspending her for the final game against the USA.

'Coming in as a 17 or 18 year old, having only ever played with guys all my life, it wasn't a huge step to play with the national team,'

While many players cleaned toilets, Salisbury worked in a chicken factory to afford the international camps.

Salisbury told Football Australia. 'But when I realised the standard of competition overseas, some of the girls in the US were phenomenal players and that was a real eye-opener for me.' Her World Cup performances earned her a glimpse

In 2007 Salisbury captained the Matildas to their fourth consecutive World Cup.

Salisbury clutches the hand of fellow immortal Melissa Barbieri at the World Cup finals.

of burgeoning semi-professional football in Japan, playing for club sides in Kyoto and Osaka for the next two years, but she broke her leg in a tour of the USA in 1996, which hampered her club career.

After the excitement of her meteoric rise she discovered the truth of women's football: despite the AIS funding she still had to pay to play for the Matildas and work to support herself while they were travelling. While many players cleaned toilets, Salisbury worked in a chicken factory to afford the international camps. She had to take four months off per year from any job she could find so she could play for Australia. She said the team 'played for the love of the game', but football took an immense toll on every aspect of her life from her body to her relationships and mental health.

The reward was that by 1998 when she was still just 24 years of age Salisbury was already mentoring a new generation of female footballers that was entering the national team as young as the age of 16. Some of them, such as future legend Heather Garriock, had posters of Salisbury's 1995 World Cup team on their bedroom walls. By this time Salisbury had played nearly 20 matches across nine countries in just two years, and to prepare for the 1999 World Cup her team entered North Korea at the height of Kim Jong Il's hermit kingdom. She played in front of 60,000 people wearing badges of their leader's face and on grass pitches that had been cut by hand.

Exotic foreign experiences became commonplace, and it was a very different Matildas team that qualified in 1999. Salisbury scored nine times in three matches as the Matildas destroyed the likes of American Samoa 21-0 and Fiji 17-0 en route to their second OFC

Salisbury's success helped pave the way for the formation of the W-League (now A-League Women) in 2008.

title, making a mockery of the competition. By the 1999 World Cup the Matildas had played nearly 60 matches in four years, and the blood, sweat and tears of that journey had turned Salisbury's team into a ruthless outfit. They were increasingly tactically astute but were famed for their aggressive, even thuggish, physicality.

Australia earned their first World Cup point in 1999 by drawing against Ghana amid six yellow cards and a send-off but lost the next two matches despite Salisbury scoring against China thanks to rash penalty-conceding tackles and a further red card. That year they returned to an Australian public in the grips of Olympic mania but which was still completely ignoring them; however, the team's relentless drive evolved. They moved into the AIS live-in facilities and began earning $200 per week, their first taste of professionalism. They took the controversial supplement creatine, started each day at 6 am and trained 14 times per week.

The Matildas were approached to do a full-frontal nude calendar to raise the team's profile and 12 of them, including Salisbury, agreed. The calendar made headlines around the world and sold prolifically, although the players only pocketed around $4,000 each. Only 1,500 fans turned up to the team's next game in Melbourne, but 10,000 cheered them on in Sydney in June when they drew 1-1 with world number two China.

In contemporary Matildas history the 2000 Olympics campaign is seen as another disappointing tournament. Salisbury's diving header against Sweden in front of 33,600 fans at the Sydney Football Stadium to score the Matildas' first Olympic goal is its most alluring memory, but for Salisbury herself her entire career now pales in comparison to the power of being an Olympian; the mere thought still gives her goosebumps. She walked out in the opening ceremony in front of 110,000 people at the Sydney Olympic Stadium for the opening ceremony and 3.7 billion television viewers around the world. 'I realised I was just this small little speck in a small little team,' she told the *Newcastle Herald*, 'part of something that was so much bigger than anything on the planet.'

Despite Salisbury's best efforts, the Matildas finished bottom of their group and had failed in the eyes of Australia's sporting administrators.

'I realised I was just this small little speck in a small little team . . . part of something that was so much bigger than anything on the planet.'

The AIS' Matildas program was axed and prospective coaches backed out of the role, before the entire Australian Women's Soccer Association dissolved. Salisbury was unemployed the moment the tournament was over, and went back to working the production line at an Adelaide factory. Once again she attempted to join male teams, but this time she was rejected. She had accomplished more than any female footballer before her but was facing worse challenges than she had had as a teenager. 'The build up was nothing like anyone had ever seen,' she told *The Sydney Morning Herald*. 'Then afterwards we were shipped off back to our home states and left for dead. We were actually gone, and forgotten.'

Australian football was imploding after the Olympics, but the US had formed the world's first professional women's league and Salisbury pioneered a pathway from Australia to the USA that, a decade later, virtually every Matilda would follow.

She says her two-year spell in the USA, particularly with New York Power, was the 'first time I'd been treated like an athlete', and she was willing to turn her back on the Matildas in the hope of a sustainable career.

Had the league survived she may have been lost to Australia forever, but its quick demise meant by 2003 she was back to humiliating Pacific opponents to qualify for the World Cup. This time the Matildas scored 45 goals in four matches, conceding none, to win Salisbury's third OFC trophy. Salisbury had spearheaded the team's evolution from being a side that couldn't qualify on home soil in 1991 to a team that was so excessively dominant they soon left the Oceania confederation altogether. The Matildas entered the first FIFA women's world rankings at 15 out of 108 teams, and Salisbury was awarded the Matildas captaincy for her efforts. She held the position for the next seven years until her retirement.

Fittingly, Salisbury captained the Matildas for the first time in the 2005 World Cup against Russia, the team she'd debuted against nearly 10 years earlier. The Brisbane park had been replaced by a new $150 million Los Angeles stadium and the parked cars had become 15,000 fans and a global television audience, but the score line, a 2-1 loss, was exactly the same. The Matildas held China to a draw but lost to Ghana to exit the tournament winless once again.

Salisbury always maintained that she was shy off the field, but her intensity in training and matches inspired Australia's best young players to a greater level. The Matildas qualified for the 2004 Athens Olympics, and Salisbury played momentously as the Matildas beat their Greek hosts for their first win at a major international tournament. 'It seems so strange, because it's been such a long time coming,' she said after the match, and she proved it in her 100th appearance six days later, drawing against world champions USA to progress to the quarter-finals. She had transformed a team of youthful prodigies such as Lisa De Vanna, Heather Garriock, Sally Shipard and Sarah Walsh into a world-class side and FIFA recognised her immense impact, naming her in its World XI for the first time.

Less than a month after the Socceroos' 2006 World Cup success the Matildas stormed to the Asian Cup final in their debut appearance, on home soil. It was a travesty that, in the midst of Australian football's moment in the spotlight, miserly attendances in Adelaide

While today's Matildas sign million-dollar Nike endorsement deals, Salisbury instead took a sales job selling Nike sneakers . . .

A rare shot from Salisbury's final Matildas match, a fairytale farewell against Italy in 2009.

witnessed the Matildas set a new precedent for national team success. Salisbury's side stated their intention from the outset, smashing Asian heavyweights South Korea 4-0 to welcome themselves to Asian football before beating Japan, Myanmar and Thailand to make the final against seven-time champions China without conceding a goal. Australia took a two-goal lead but was pegged back by their old enemy, and Australia's cool-headed captain – who had spent her teenage years demanding to take penalties from older boys – watched from the sidelines as Australia lost in the shoot-out. She almost certainly would have taken the crucial fifth spot kick; however, Australia missed their third and fourth and handed China the win.

The Matildas had nevertheless cemented themselves as a global football heavyweight on home soil, but the Australian media almost entirely ignored them. While today's Matildas sign million-dollar Nike endorsement deals, Salisbury instead took a sales job selling Nike sneakers – yet her sentiments post-match were serene: 'We just thought we were better than we were.'

In 2007 Salisbury captained the Matildas to their fourth straight World Cup, breaking new territory at 33 years of age. Her herculean physique had endured hundreds of brutal football matches, 13 years of global travel and laborious day jobs without the sports scientists and physiotherapists of her Socceroos peers. Every time she left the pitch she could feel the straining tissue in her calves and the grinding sliver of cartilage in her knees. Now she was up against a new generation of female footballers more technically gifted than the world had ever seen.

It was here that Salisbury truly cemented herself as the Matildas' greatest ever leader: she dictated Australia's quick tempo as they ran riot against Ghana, winning their first match at a World Cup 4-1. She then marshalled a resolute Australian defence against world number four Norway before launching her own series of attacks to shift the momentum and secure a 1-1 draw. Finally, she delivered the moment against Canada that defined an emphatic career. The Matildas made their first World Cup quarter-final against Brazil, but Salisbury had given everything. She left the field injured after 20 minutes and her team couldn't quite hold on without her. She was named in FIFA's World XI for the second time, but now she returned

The success of Salisbury's Matildas demanded Australia's attention, and the next year the A-League Women was born.

home to mass media coverage and a hero's welcome.

The success of Salisbury's Matildas demanded Australia's attention, and the next year the A-League Women was born. It launched an era of professionalism she'd fought for her entire life, and she ended her career captaining her home-town club. At her 2009 retirement she held the record for the most Matildas appearances and goals, and she had played for the Matildas in every FIFA competition in the team's history.

National career		
Years	Appearances (B*)	Goals
1994–2009	151 (171)	38
Club career**			
---	---	---	---
Years	Team	Appearances	Goals
1995–1996	Panasonic Bambina	–	–
1997	Takarazuka Bunnys	–	–
2002	Memphis Mercury	–	–
2003	New York Power	13	3
2008–2010	Newcastle Jets	7	1

Honours	
Oceania Football Confederation Nations Cup	1994, 1998, 2003
FIFA World XI	2004, 2007
Football Federation Australia Hall of Fame	2009
Australia's Greatest Female Player	2014
Alex Tobin Medal	2017
Sport Australia Hall of Fame	2019

* Total caps including exhibition, friendlies and other (B) games.
** Not all appearances and goals have been recorded.

Johnny Warren at the 1974 World Cup. He was the public face of Australian soccer for decades.

JOHNNY WARREN

Birthdate	17 May 1943
Place of birth	Sydney, New South Wales
Major teams	Australia, Canterbury-Marrickville, St George Budapest
Position	Midfielder

The man known as 'Captain Socceroo' is the most pivotal figure in Australian football history. His revolutionary passion provided Australia's voice in the global game.

With a single utterance Johnny Warren encapsulated the agony and ecstasy; the moment that defines him is the moment that defines Australian football. He captained Australia to its first international trophy in 1967 and its first World Cup in 1974, and played in its first World Cup match. He won four New South Wales state championships, his final as the team's player and coach, and he even scored the winning goal in the grand final before substituting himself, but off the field he was one of the most influential footballing figures of the 20th century. He wasn't just a player, captain and coach but also a journalist, administrator, author, broadcaster, lobbyist and revolutionary. When asked what his defining legacy should be weeks before his death his response was: 'I told you so.' The defining moments of every other footballer in this book are evidence he was correct.

Warren entered Australian football in the midst of a revolution and left in the midst of one. Born in 1943, he was the youngest of three boys in a sixth-generation, quintessentially Australian family that lived metres away from where Captain Cook's first fleet arrived in Botany Bay. As his ocker autobiography *Sheilas, Wogs and Poofters* makes clear Warren wasn't born into football like the European migrants who dominate Australian teams, but his love ran much deeper than Australia's cultural divide.

Warren's agility and determination on display playing for St George Budapest in 1968.

He and his brothers Geoff and Ross were typically competitive young boys at a time when street cricket on quiet cul-de-sacs was the rite of passage. 'Wogball', as it was widely derided, may never have entered his consciousness if it hadn't been for a chance visit to watch Croatian club Hadjuk Split – on tour for the city's booming and fanatical Slavic population – play in Sydney. At only six years of age Warren couldn't have realised what hooked him that day, but while he and his brothers were excelling in the suburb's homogenous soccer tedium for teams such as the Botany Methodists and Protestant Churches, he knew a crucible of real football passion was

Warren at a football clinic in 1969, both a literal and figurative football mentor.

By 1959 when he was aged 15, Warren had joined Australia's best and oldest football club, Canterbury, in the closest thing apathetic Australia had to an organised competition.

bubbling beneath Sydney's surface and that it was about to erupt.

By 1959 when he was aged 15, Warren had joined Australia's best and oldest football club, Canterbury, in the closest thing apathetic Australia had to an organised competition. Australia had just joined FIFA, but the Australian Soccer Football Association (ASFA) – its name an example of its hamstrung interests – was still a stagnant outpost of the English FA and had an amateur board and no national league to officiate, which meant its focus was centred on the New South Wales First Division. By then more than a million post-war immigrants had arrived in Australia from Europe's football heartlands, but nearly two decades before the end of the White Australia policy the ASFA's focus was on ensuring the amateur New South Wales first tier remained a whitewashed suburban relic. This forced émigrés to build their

Warren's focus was always firmly on the boundless potential of Australian football.

own community clubs from the ground up, which they did in spades.

The migrant-backed clubs were blocked from the first tier but made the New South Wales second division into a vibrant, multicultural league. While first division clubs could barely muster 800 people to Sydney stadiums, second-tier sides were attracting 8,000 fans to suburban parks and generating so much revenue they were starting to pay their players. When these increasingly powerful migrant clubs continued to be blocked the revolution began: their owners formed a rebel administration and attracted big deferrers, including

Warren at a football clinic in Liverpool, NSW in 1970.

> **He'd lash out at an opponent if he thought he'd been wronged, but he was just as quick to turn the other cheek if he'd been decked by a stronger man.**

Warren's powerhouse Canterbury, to a breakaway league. There Warren was quickly moulded into a decisive, tactical midfielder by former Hungarian national team performance coach Joseph Vlasits. By 1960 17-year-old Warren had become a starlet in New South Wales's new league, and he scored two crucial goals in a 3-2 semi-final win against APIA as Canterbury won the 1960 New South Wales grand final.

Over the next two years Warren spearheaded Canterbury's dominance and became a commanding yet graceful midfielder with the testament grit and determination that would hallmark his playing career. He had cool, piercing eyes that radiated intelligence, hinting at the mercurial football brain that hid behind them, and a studious, thoughtful demeanour that drew him to the game's most tactical positions.

He was small and of average build, at just 175 centimetres, but he was tough – never shying away from a challenge – and fair. He'd lash out at an opponent if he thought he'd been wronged, but he was just as quick to turn the other cheek if he'd been decked by a stronger man. His stature and speed made him elegant on the ball, gliding in possession with his head held high and always quick to spot the dutiful lay-off, but he was a ruthless competitor above all else and usually played with a notable grimace slashed across his face.

Vlasits had moved to St George Budapest and helped turn the club into one of the nation's biggest, so Warren and his brother Ross also moved there in 1963. Warren added an impressive shooting ability to his wide-ranging arsenal at St George and established himself as one of Australia's finest midfielders. A natural leader, he was not only named club captain but he took over marketing and promotion for the club. Beyond New South Wales, an Australian national team was almost non-existent: Australia had only ever played sporadic friendly matches before the 1956 Melbourne Olympics gave the team a chance for international recognition. Their failure had relegated the team to international purgatory, and by 1965 Australia hadn't played another country in seven years.

That year, under the guise of football's new power brokers, Australia was revived to compete in their first World Cup campaign under their first permanent coach, Tiko Jelisavčić. Twenty-two-year-old Warren was called up to the squad but was left out for both qualifiers as Australia was dismantled by North Korea and dumped out of qualifying. It was a nightmare: the Australians hated Jelisavčić and were ridden with diarrhoea and other illnesses from their first trip abroad. Warren witnessed Australia's disastrous reintroduction to global football from the sidelines, but here in the stench, hatred and humidity was the real beginning of the Socceroos.

Jelisavčić turned to Warren to remedy Australia's disorganised midfield, and he started his international debut against Cambodia two days later in front of 20,000 hostile fans in Phnom Penh and had an instantly calming effect. Australia's results improved markedly with Warren but the baptism of fire continued: in just his third match, against Taiwan, the game descended into a riot. Taiwanese fans stormed

> **They fled back to their hotel and hid under the tables while fans threw rocks through their windows.**

the team's dressing room and Warren and his teammates were narrowly saved by riot police. They fled back to their hotel and hid under the tables while fans threw rocks through their windows.

Warren was reunited with Vlasits when the latter took charge of the national team in 1967, and his team was handed the greatest test of its career. The Socceroos were heading to war, at the bloodiest height of Vietnam, as a propaganda exercise to support the Australian troops. The South Vietnam Independence Cup had been held in Saigon each year since 1961, but the Australian military had arranged Australia and New Zealand's involvement as a public relations exercise. It was the third tournament in Australia's history, and the team had only played four competitive matches. Warren didn't realise he had been 'blindly steered' into propaganda until years later, but the seriousness of their situation was immediately obvious: 'I can remember some of

Warren, bottom right, with the Socceroos' pioneering 1974 World Cup team.

us playing billiards in the mess hall one night when we suddenly heard machine guns firing,' Warren wrote in his autobiography. 'All of the players were under the table in the blink of an eye.'

Soon after they arrived Viet Cong soldiers were caught breaking into the hotel with explosives. Australia's training base was next to a minefield and it was the middle of the monsoon season, so the Socceroos trained on the roof of their hotel, where players would also go at night to watch the aerial bombs exploding in the distance. The hotel's owner had stolen their food vouchers, leaving the entire team eating 'substitute ham', and Warren's teammate Stan Ackerley was hurtled across the room when he was electrocuted by a power socket. Soldiers with mine detectors walked through the stands during matches, but in the middle of this hell – at 25 years of age and with just six international appearances – Vlasits thrust the Socceroos captaincy onto Warren's shoulders. At night Warren slept near the shower, the safest place during an attack, but during the day it was his responsibility to guide the young Australian team – whose members' average age was just 22 and many of whom had friends fighting in the war – to prove that Australian football could be taken seriously, in the most horrendous of conditions. His captaincy proved to be an incredibly apt decision.

Warren played every minute of every match. He scored in the opener as Australia beat New Zealand 5-3, then scored again in the second game to beat the South Vietnamese 1-0 in

Warren shakes hands with short-lived Socceroos coach Rudi Gutendorf in 1980.

> 'It was one of those moments that I knew I was going to remember for the rest of my life.'

front of 40,000 fans. Once again riots ensued, and tear gas streamed onto the pitch. South Vietnam's president visited his national team at half-time to offer them money if they won, but there was no stopping Warren's side. They smashed Singapore 5-1 and scraped past Malaysia 1-0 in the midst of more on-pitch brawls and crowd violence for a shot at Australia's first international trophy in the final against South Korea. At home the tournament was almost completely ignored, but when Warren led Australia onto the pitch for that final match the crowd that had been so hostile up to that point were cheering them on like the home side. 'I can still remember the sensation of hairs standing up on the back of my neck as I stood in the tunnel,' Warren wrote. Composed as ever, he scored the crucial go-ahead goal and steered his side to a 3-2 win. 'It was one of those moments that I knew I was going to remember for the rest of my life.'

Warren and his teammates, who had to take annual leave from their day jobs to take part, were paid $50 per week for their services, and because they won the tournament they were allowed to keep their tracksuits. Warren was aged 25, an amateur two years into his national career, and he and his team had been spat at, cheated, sickened, pelted with bottles, nails and rocks, had their legs broken and their dressing rooms stormed and their hotels bombed and shot at. They'd survived multiple war zones, attempted murders, snakes, food poisoning and electrocutions. Barely anyone cared, and many back home actively derided them. They had done it all while sacrificing money, opportunities and relationships to the detriment of day jobs and young families.

The Socceroos' first trophy was a watershed moment for Australian football, and it began the greatest period in Warren's career. By the end of 1967 he was the most important player in the national team and had played 14 of their 16 matches since his debut. He'd led Australia to success on the world stage, and now back home at St George he was glimpsing how phenomenal football in Australia could be. St George was a stable, successful club and a pillar of their community, even operating their own licensed bar and venue. Rather than rest on their laurels, however, the club always wanted more. In Warren's first six seasons they made five grand finals but lost four of them, and finished league runners-up five times.

The near misses ignited a burning ambition, and at a time when many Australian teams were delighted to lure ageing émigrés St George developed their own football talent. They cycled through coaches in search of a true innovator, and found two consecutively in future Socceroos coaches Frank Arok and Rale Rasic. Both coaches demanded a new level of discipline and professionalism, implementing modern training methods and controlling their players on and off the pitch. Warren called Arok the 'first real manager in Australian club history' and became increasingly confident and skilful in possession, developing a trademark array of feints he used to devastating attacking effect. St George was one of the country's most dominant teams for Warren's 11-year spell, and he guided the club to three New South Wales titles and six grand finals and two Federation Cups.

In 1965 Australia only had to beat one opponent to qualify for the World Cup, and they'd failed. In 1969 they had to beat four across nine games, but Warren's public

They flew to Africa for a play-off against Rhodesia, and it's there that Warren's story becomes a little unusual.

demands for greater support were beginning to have an effect. Over 30,000 people watched Australia beat Greece in Sydney that year, sending Warren's side into qualification on a high. The squad of part timers left a scorching Sydney summer on a 20-hour flight to freezing Seoul, but three days later they beat Japan and South Korea back to back – again to smashed bottles and a police escort.

They flew to Africa for a play-off against Rhodesia, and it's there that Warren's story becomes a little unusual. He was ruled out sick from the first match and a wayward Australia struggled through two stagnant draws, and the story goes that the Australians hired a witch doctor on the advice of a local journalist to curse the Rhodesians. Warren dominated the next match, scoring in a 3-1 win to send Australia through. The spell caster demanded $1,000 payment but the Australians refused and left the country, and the furious shaman cursed the Socceroos. Whether the story is

Mr and Mrs Soccer – Les Murray and Warren – with Tracey Holmes in 1998.

true or not, Warren believed it wholeheartedly and Australia lost both their final qualifiers against Israel to end their World Cup hopes.

Back home in 1971, Warren captained St George to his second Australian football milestone when they were invited to an international tournament in Tokyo against Japan's senior and reserve national sides and Danish club champions BK Frem. He led St George to a draw with Japan, thrashed the Danes 3-0 and then destroyed Japan's reserves 6-2 to win the tournament in style. As captain Warren had now won the first international trophy for an Australian club and for the Australian national team, but that same year he suffered an innocuous knee knock for St George that tore his anterior cruciate ligament (ACL) and shattered his career at its peak. It was a devastating injury that semi-professional players rarely returned from in the 1970s, but after 15 months of rehabilitation he fought to return to the Socceroos. Rasic had replaced Vlasits as national coach and believed the ACL tear had weakened Warren as a player. Fearsome defender Peter Wilson had taken his captaincy and Warren's midfield role was usurped by Jimmy Mackay, who was the same age and also had a thunderbolt shot in his arsenal.

After playing 29 of the Socceroos' previous 34 matches, Warren appeared in just eight of their next 19 before his retirement. His impact had already been widely acknowledged – he received a Member of the British Empire award in 2003 – and it was hard to believe he could be replaced, but Rasic was the strongest-willed coach Australia had ever had,

Johnny Warren · 61

a trait that got him sacked by Soccer Australia immediately after the 1974 World Cup. Warren sat on the bench as a Mackay thunderbolt against South Korea secured Australia's first qualification for the 1974 World Cup.

By then 31 years of age, Warren played just 44 minutes of Australia's four warm-up friendlies but, given his extraordinary achievements to make it this far, few were surprised when he walked out onto the pitch to start Australia's first World Cup match against East Germany in Hamburg in front of hundreds of millions of television viewers

Warren and Murray in 2002. The pair were the voice of Australian football for decades.

> Leading until the end, he substituted himself off the pitch, ensuring his own fairy-tale finish.

across the world. Australia had never played a team of this calibre, let alone on such a momentous occasion, but they exhibited the same grit and determination that Warren had instilled in the side in Vietnam. For Warren, however, the curse returned: he suffered a nasty foot injury against the East Germans, and while he endured to finish the game it was the last match he ever played for the Socceroos.

Warren returned from the World Cup to find St George near the bottom of the ladder, and he took over the coaching reins in addition to captaining the side. He commanded a startling turnaround and his side won eight of their last nine matches to make the grand final, in front of a boisterous Sydney crowd. In the final stages he dispossessed an opponent in the central circle and feinted and burst past another defender before scoring the winner with the outside of his foot from the edge of the box. Leading until the end, he substituted himself off the pitch, ensuring his own fairy-tale finish.

Although Warren's playing career was over, his football legacy had just begun. The irony of his autobiographical title is that Australian football in the 1960s and 1970s was populated by some of the fiercest athletes Australian sport has ever seen: émigrés from war-torn Europe and hardened Brits spat out by the English football system, all thrown together on sun-baked pitches with little control or volition. He dedicated himself to shifting Australian football's reputation and encouraging the next generation and helped establish and then coach a football club in Canberra, where he ran famed training camps for Australian youth.

His greatest impact came at SBS, where he and broadcast partner Les Murray, nicknamed 'Mr and Mrs Soccer', became the public faces of Australian football for three decades. Warren was an astute analyst, passionate commentator and tireless advocate who legitimised Australian football to the masses. He hosted the television program *Captain Socceroo*, which inspired many of the Socceroos' future golden generation, and wrote or contributed to eight books on football in addition to weekly newspaper columns. His crying on live television after the Socceroos' disastrous loss to Iran in 1998 symbolised the suffering of all Australian football fans.

'He was the embodiment of Australian soccer's struggle and the struggle of life,' Andy Harper told *The Sydney Morning Herald*. 'He demystified multiculturalism for Australia and opened up corners of the world that Australians didn't even know existed.'

Warren was diagnosed with lung cancer in 2002, the same year he delivered one of his greatest legacies: the Report of the NSW Premier's Soccer Taskforce. After three months of writing he listed 11 recommendations, from as symbolic as calling the game football to as major as establishing the A-League. These recommendations became the foundation of the 2003 Crawford Report, a federal government investigation into the systemic corruption and mismanagement of Soccer Australia. Warren was the only football-related member of the committee. The Australian Sports Commission threatened to withdraw funding for the organisation, and the resulting changes were tremendous. The Soccer Australia board retired en masse and Football Australia was born.

A frail Warren was presented with FIFA's Centennial Order

> 'He demystified multiculturalism for Australia and opened up corners of the world that Australians didn't even know existed.'

of Merit in 2004 alongside Pele and Franz Beckenbauer. His last public appearance was at the announcement of the A-League in April 2004. He died seven months later, exactly 12 months before the Socceroos qualified for their first World Cup in 32 years in front of 86,000 fans and a giant banner reading 'I told you so'.

National career		
Years	Appearances	Goals
1965–1974	42	7

Club career*			
Years	Team	Appearances	Goals
1959–1962	Canterbury Marrickville	–	–
1963–1964	St George Budapest	–	–
1964	Stockport County	0	0
1965–1974	St George Budapest	200+	–

Honours	
New South Wales First Division	1960, 1967, 1971, 1974
Federation Cup	1964, 1972
Member of the Order of the British Empire	1974
Sport Australia Hall of Fame	1988
Football Federation Australia Hall of Fame	1999
Australian Sports Medal	2000
Australian Centenary Medal	2001
Order of Australia	2002
FIFA Centennial Order of Merit	2004
Alex Tobin Medal	2008

Not all appearances and goals have been recorded.

Julie Dolan captaining Australia in its first official female match against New Zealand at Seymour Park in 1979.

JULIE DOLAN

Birthdate	5 January 1961
Place of birth	Sutherland, New South Wales
Major teams	Australia, New South Wales, St George Budapest
Position	Midfielder

No Australian athlete has created a greater legacy from a humbler outset than Julie Dolan. Her ubiquitous trailblazing helped pave the way for professional women's sport in Australia.

'The ball came from midfield and travelled out to Carol Vinson on the wing. She crossed it over to Janine Riddington, who was flying up the middle of the park. The ball had beaten the Brazilian backline, Riddington was on the ball and Brazil's goalkeeper was suddenly the last line of defence. She had come out a long way trying to stop her, and Riddo just chipped it over her head. It was just . . . beautiful.

'I look back at the team performance now and it was just tremendous. The team [was] buzzing, as I should have been – it was the most incredible goal I've ever seen. Everybody had a right to be buzzing but my emotions were flat that day. We were just in survival mode for a little too long. We scraped the win – that was my feeling at the time – because it was such a tough game. Looking back, I know that's why I was a leader. I knew that about myself and I guess that's why I was recognised by the coaches who made me captain. It's difficult to actually say that though. You know it about yourself . . . but you don't know how other people view you.'

Julie Dolan is Matildas cap number one, the first Australian woman to walk onto a football pitch representing her nation in an official international football match. She captained Australia's women's national team in the first women's World Cup, Asian Cup and Oceanian Cup in history, and she also captained Australia in their first international tournament, pioneered the first female football league and spearheaded the most dominant Australian club team of all time. Her impact was so momentous that the year she retired the Julie Dolan Medal for the best female footballer of the year was created in her honour. In 2000 the International Federation of Football History and Statistics named her Oceania's Female Player of the Century.

Dolan's career had the humblest of beginnings. She was born in January 1961, the single girl to four brothers, in a suburban backyard in Sydney's Sutherland Shire. Her rough and tumble upbringing is still evident in the way she speaks and the way she coaches young girls today: there's not an ounce of fragility in female football's pioneer. 'Girls didn't play football back then but my upbringing was very different,' she said. 'We just

Dolan, centre left, captained Australia at the 1984 Taiwan Invitational.

> **Her club played seven years undefeated from 1971 to 1977 in Australia's first female football league . . .**

played football in the backyard all the time and that's where it all started. The girls at school didn't play football so then I played football at school with the boys as well. You can't beat that sort of training.'

Dolan was so talented that by 10 years of age she became involved with Australia's leading football club at the time, St George Budapest. St George's men's side was captained by Australian football's other iconoclast, Johnny Warren, who welcomed the formation of the club's first female team. St George was a radiating pioneer at this time – even Les Murray played there as a junior – but Dolan and Warren became the greatest: they nurtured Australian football from its infancy, and their passion and expertise for the game and its history still reverberates around Australian lounge rooms, television studios and packed stadiums every time the Socceroos and Matildas take to the pitch. The pair's lasting legacy will be forever intertwined, as Australian football's awards night is called the Dolan Warren Awards in their honour.

The St George Budapest women's football team is the most successful football team in Australian history and quite possibly the most dominant team of any code. It was the first female side to demand professionalism and dedication from its players, which perfectly complemented Dolan's prodigious enthusiasm. She was playing against hardened female athletes in their 30s, but after years of tussling it out with her older brothers she was far readier than anyone expected. Even as a pre-teen Dolan was quick, hard tempered and extremely determined, and her incredible success at such a young age is one of her most startling achievements. Her club played seven years undefeated from 1971 to 1977 in Australia's first female football league, New South Wales's Metropolitan Ladies Soccer Association (MLSA). In 1972 alone they scored 206 goals and conceded none.

In 1974 when Dolan was 14 years of age and had already been playing in the MLSA for three years the Australian Women's Soccer Association (AWSA) was founded, which led to the formation of the first National Women's Soccer

Championship in 1974. Australia's governing body had little interest in female football, so the AWSA took it upon themselves to provide national opportunities for the game's burgeoning talent pool. Dolan captained New South Wales's first female state team to win the inaugural tournament – the first of many – which set the precedent for the first Australian national team.

Asia was faster than their European counterparts to organise international tournaments, thanks in part to pressure from advocates in Australia and New Zealand. The first women's Asian Cup was originally slated to be a tournament between women's clubs to feature St George, but the Australian Football Confederation (AFC) soon realised they could make it a fully fledged international tournament. Thailand, Malaysia, Singapore, Hong Kong and New Zealand all sent their first official national teams to the historic tournament, but FIFA didn't recognise the AWSA thanks to the discrimination inherent in Australian football's nightmare bureaucracy.

This means the first Australian women's national team to play in a FIFA tournament are excluded from the rest of 'official' Matildas history, a hideous quirk that surmises the

> 'I was the engine room, I could direct play, my job was to be there in defence and then be there in attack.'

struggles they faced at the time. But to 14-year-old Dolan it didn't matter at all: she was suddenly on a plane to Hong Kong with a team of women from New South Wales working part-time jobs to make global football history at the 1975 AFC Women's Championship, more than 40 years before the Socceroos played at their first Asian Cup. Dolan dominated as Australia made the semi-finals and was named in the tournament's Asian All Star Team. 'Back in those days 14 year olds just didn't get on planes and go to Hong Kong,' Dolan laughed. 'That was extraordinary in itself: to find myself on a plane, representing Australia in a handpicked team, wearing the Australian colours. We were representing our country. It was an incredible experience to be involved at that level of the sport, playing international games.

'It's really hard to say what kind of player I was,' she continued. 'These days people can see themselves on film, they're shown how they perform on the park. I knew I could play, and that I could compete on the world stage, but I didn't know if I was a class above anybody else or where I sat on that particular spectrum. I was just confident about my game in general. I was the engine room, I could direct play, my job was to be there in defence and then be there in attack. I had an incredible stamina, so that was a job that I could do very well.'

Dolan was a star, although her umbra was still limited to a rather small raggle of football-mad pioneers in the bucolic Sydney suburbs.

However, this was soon to change, as equal rights legislation and a strong health and fitness movement led to a huge influx of female sports participation in the 1970s. For the first time it was seen as necessary to encourage women into sport, and while attempts to hold a women's World Cup had emerged before in Europe and America they had failed to gain traction. Ultimately, it was Asia that succeeded.

In 1978 the first Women's World Invitational Tournament – the pilot tournament for FIFA's Women's

Dolan washes cars with her Australian teammates as a fundraiser so they could play at the 1975 AFC Women's Championship.

Dolan strikes the ball against New Zealand in that groundbreaking 1979 match.

World Cup – was held in Taiwan. It was small and a little strange, but it was grandiose: teams came from Australia, Germany, the USA, Finland, France, China, Austria, Denmark, Sweden, Polynesia, Switzerland, Canada, England and Thailand. Some teams were supported by burgeoning national federations, while others were club sides that paid their own airfares. Every player was an international pioneer and they were treated like heroes by the Taiwanese. These invitational tournaments grew to feature grand opening ceremonies with gymnastic drills and military regattas while thousands of Taiwanese children packed the stands, exhibiting tifo arrays. It's almost unimaginable now what it was like for Dolan to step off the plane in Taiwan, still aged just 17, and be transported from a dusty suburban pitch in Illawarra to being a football star on the world stage.

Dolan starred in every match as Australia performed admirably, thrashing Thailand 5-0 and beating the Austrians, drawing against Denmark and a US team and losing narrowly to the Swedes. 'I think the relationship with Soccer Australia was always "Okay, well, there's the men's game, and then the girls have a go",' Dolan said. 'There's always a disparity between men's and women's sport; that hasn't changed. But in terms of travelling abroad, the foreign countries, their teams and their associations welcomed us like royalty, which was something completely new for us. There were always people packed at the airport to greet us and check us out. The accommodation was always top notch. We were treated a lot differently. We never experienced that treatment in Australia, but it's not something you look for if you've never experienced it.'

It was members of the Oceania Football Confederation (OFC) who helped convince FIFA executives to form an official women's World Cup, and by 1979 Australia's governing body was suddenly playing catch up with its own figureheads. While they wouldn't be called the Matildas until SBS held a 1995 public vote, Australia's governing body formed the first official Australian women's football team in 1979. Dolan had just turned 18, but she was named the first Australian women's captain ahead of many women her senior. Barely adult, she was a born leader and had garnered the respect of much older teammates. She had also already experienced a glimmer of the organisation and fanfare for women's football that the broader Australian public wouldn't experience until decades later.

'It was a diverse group of players,' Dolan said, 'players with their own level of training and coaching, coming in from different states to an emerging scenario. But as Australians do, they always make up for it. We recognised the

Dolan, standing right of centre, at FIFA's pilot Women's World Cup tournament in 1988.

importance, especially in the sense that each time that we played, and each tournament we entered, was a roadmap to something bigger. We didn't know how big or how much better, but we were definitely on the road to something special.'

The first ever official Matildas match was against New Zealand – as the next seven would be – because there was still no funding for the team. Far from the relative glories of Taiwan, Sydney's Seymour Shaw Park near Dolan's home suburb hosted the history-making match on a suburban ground with rows of wooden planks propped up on scaffolding as the stands. Dolan and her teammates walked door to door handing out flyers as the media didn't care, and apart from family and friends there was almost no one in attendance. She even sewed her own badges onto her kit but it was an official Australian kit nonetheless, and the 2-2 draw was the formal beginning of an extremely proud history.

Dolan captained Australia's first official 10 matches, only one of which they lost, before captaining the side in their first official international tournament: the inaugural OFC Women's Nations Cup. Dolan led by example

The opening ceremony cost over 11 million New Taiwan dollars to stage and featured 6,300 male and female performers conducting dragon dances in front of 28,000 fans.

in Australia's first taste of FIFA competition, scoring three times as her side made the final only to lose it to New Zealand in extra time.

Australia had to wait until 1984 to compete internationally again but would do so in two successive tournaments. They began at China's Xian International Tournament, beating two Chinese sides and a US team, with Dolan scoring the winner. They then played at the extraordinary 1984 Taiwan Invitational, which had taken six years to organise but was worth the wait. The opening ceremony cost over 11 million New Taiwan dollars to stage and featured 6,300 male and female performers conducting dragon dances in front of 28,000 fans. Dolan was then 23 years of age and her Australian side was never going to be overawed by the occasion. She captained Australia in every match, commanding them to

Dolan was key in trailblazing a pathway for all Australian female sporting teams to follow.

victory against US and Norwegian teams as well as draws against the Germans and Japan.

'The team [was] quite organised thanks to our coach Jim Selby,' Dolan said. 'We travelled out to Camden to spend five days training every day as a team; it was a very professional, refined level of coaching. In terms of preparing for games, we really couldn't have done better. You see the girls going into training camps these days and there is a lot more consideration, there are a lot more personnel around them, it's a lot fancier. But it's really not that different from what we experienced; we just lacked the trimmings.'

Dolan made 18 FIFA-recognised international appearances in a 10-year international career but actually played for Australia 34 times. Most of the greatest spectacles over those years took place in unofficial internationals – FIFA's extraordinary pilot tournaments – and often in front of record crowds, but despite the professional level of training that sympathetic clubs, sponsors and passionate volunteers were able to offer the players still had day jobs that often had to take priority. 'You came back home, and if you still had a job then you went off,' Dolan says. 'I did all sorts of work because sometimes they would keep me employed while I played, sometimes they didn't.' As she struggled to provide for herself, Australia struggled without her. She missed many Australian national opportunities, most notably the 1986 OFC Championship. Australia was a shadow of itself without her and lost twice to Taiwan.

Dolan made a triumphant return for female football's watershed moment when FIFA held its first women's World Cup in China in 1988. It was called the 1988 FIFA Women's Invitation Tournament and the structure was closely modelled on Taiwan's success, but FIFA recognition upped the ante. Teams from every confederation took part: Ivory Coast from Africa; China, Japan and Thailand from Asia; Brazil from South America; Czechoslovakia, the Netherlands, Norway and Sweden from Europe; Canada and the USA from North America; and Australia from Oceania. Dolan's team always knew they were creating something bigger than themselves, but their blood, sweat and tears hadn't just pioneered women's football in Australia: their talent and professionalism in the first organised women's tournaments in China, Taiwan and Hong Kong had set the framework and inspired power brokers across Asia and Oceania and then FIFA itself.

The 2019 Women's World Cup drew 1.12 billion television viewers and over a million attendees, but it all started on 1 June 1988 when Dolan marched Australia out against Brazil in Jiangmen. 'Everyone was nervous, but that was channelled into energy when the game started,' she said. 'You go out

Dolan, standing third from right in the top row, led legendary teams with the likes of Joanne Millman and Cindy Heydon.

Dolan's pioneering role in Matildas history was acknowledged with a flood of awards following her retirement.

there and you're so focused, you're in the game, you're not thinking about the crowd. Everyone knew that this was going to be one of the toughest matches we ever played, and everybody went above and beyond in that game to come away with a win.'

Riddington's exceptional goal against Brazil and Dolan's astute tactical game plan saw Australia shock the world with a 1-0 win: a perfect start. Their next match was just two days later against Thailand, and the Australians had next to no conditioning. It was the midst of the monsoon season but the Thais were perfectly acclimatised to Jiangmen's stifling humidity, so Dolan knew she had to lead by example. She scored a phenomenal opening goal to set Australia running and inspire similar strikes from fellow pioneers Julie Murray and Carol Vinson, as Australia thrashed Thailand 3-0. Two straight wins assured Australia's qualification from their group for the quarter-finals, but Dolan is still not quite sure what happened against the hosts as Australia was thrashed by China at the brand new 54,000 capacity Tianhe Stadium in Guangdong.

'We got hammered by China,' Dolan laughed. 'And, you know, still to this day, I'm not really sure why that happened. Because they certainly weren't that much better than us. They definitely were the better team and the better drilled team on the day, but to lose by that much was not a good indicator of how good our team was.' It was her last tournament for Australia: 'While I played football I worked away at anything I could get with no career focus,' she said. 'I reached 28 years old and realised all I had was a pair of old football boots. So I had to go off and make a living.'

Julie Dolan · 77

Dolan retired having immeasurably transformed women's football. While she never gained professionalism during her playing career, her post-career life has vastly rewarded her talent. She became an extremely influential football administrator and an ambassador for Football Australia, and she currently guides the next generation at Australia's International Football School as technical director and director of sport. 'By the end of my career there was a lot more recognition, more media coverage and a little more acceptance of women playing football,' she reflected. 'Competitions were much more organised and we had the introduction of formal leagues; it was a massive growth. The Cheryl Salisbury era afterwards was an indication of how far the game had come, and it's since reached an extraordinary level.'

Dolan's career laid the foundations for the Matildas and A-League Women, which have both subsequently pioneered the professionalisation of Australian women's sport. However, Dolan's greatest legacy is still to come. When Australia and New Zealand host the 2023 Women's World Cup it won't just be Dolan who was there at the beginning – it will be Dolan who made it possible in the first place. It will be a time for reflection and celebration about how far Australian women's football has come but, as always, Dolan is more focused on the future: 'I see the kids at school here and I think they need to realise that no matter what, from the early days of the Matildas, even to now, you do whatever it takes to succeed,' she said. 'We used to work full-time jobs and sell raffle tickets, but these days players need to work harder than ever otherwise you don't make it. That's been the standout characteristic of Matildas players throughout history: they have always done whatever it takes.'

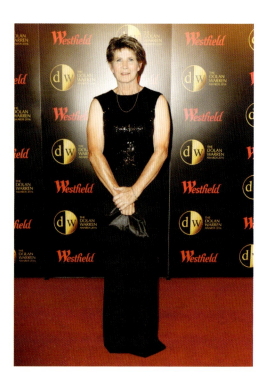

Dolan in 2016 at the annual football awards ceremony named in her honour.

The Immortals of Australian Soccer · 78

National career		
Years	Appearances (B*)	Goals
1978–1988	18 (34)	4
Club career**			
Years	Team	Appearances	Goals
1974–1988	St George Budapest, Marconi Stallions	–	–
1977–1986	New South Wales	–	–
Honours			
Julie Dolan Medal			1988
Medal of Excellence			1999
Football Federation Australia Hall of Fame			1999
Queen Elizabeth II Australian Sports Medal			1999
Oceania Player of the Century			2000
Order of Australia			2018

* Total caps including exhibition, friendlies and other (B) games.
** Not all appearances and goals have been recorded.

The Wizard of Oz, Harry Kewell, playing for the Socceroos in 2010.

HARRY KEWELL

Birthdate	22 September 1978
Place of birth	Sydney, New South Wales
Major teams	Australia, Leeds United, Liverpool, Galatasaray SK, Melbourne Victory
Position	Forward, winger, midfielder

Kewell's unprecedented talent dared Australia to dream before revealing the harrowing nightmares football can entail. History's most talented Socceroo has the nation's most complicated legacy.

Fifteen minutes remained of the wildest 90 minutes in Australian football history and it was turning into a bloodbath. The Socceroos either had to score or board the next flight to Sydney, and if they missed emerging whispers of a 'golden generation' would remain just that: an aide-memoire of what might have been. Croatian fans packed into Gottlieb-Daimler-Stadion screeched relentlessly, filling the air with a noxious white noise whenever Australia had the ball. A blurring display of yellow and red cards amplified the jeering: this match was so uncontrollable its referee retired in humiliation.

Ordinarily, introducing Harry Kewell to this dogfight would be like bringing a Maserati to the Dakar Rally, but on this night the fragile Liverpool magician was Australia's prodigal son. For 70 minutes Kewell had been devastating: firing howitzers, setting combinations, hacking legs and shoving opponents. The clock ticked over the 79th minute, and Kewell drifted to the very edge of the opposite touchline and slowed almost to a standstill until his marker, Dario Srnja, lost him entirely. There he waited patiently until Mark Bresciano received the ball on the right side.

Only the Socceroos recognised what happened next: Kewell's

patented shift to the left, the in-step foreshadowing one of his curvaceous crosses. It took two crucial seconds for Srnja to realise that Kewell was suddenly sprinting behind him, but by then it was too late. John Aloisi's head flicked the cross straight onto the most accomplished left foot in Australian history, Kewell instantly lifted the ball to stomach height and in a split second volleyed it with his right. It was in the back of the net before the goalkeeper could raise his hands.

'When it's gone past the keeper you just know,' Kewell told FIFA. 'I was already off without the ball going in the back of the net. The euphoria that comes over you is phenomenal; it goes down in Australian history as the goal that got us through to the last 16.' The Socceroos were in the knockout stages of the World Cup and the most talented yet maligned footballer Australia has ever produced was finally the hero. 'It had to be Harry,' Simon Hill famously bellowed to 6.5 million Australians watching back home. But from this day forward it rarely was Harry again.

Kewell was just 15 when he left Australia, bought by Leeds United for a $2,600 compensation payment

Kewell during a training clinic at Glenwood in 1998 while at Leeds United.

Kewell playing for Liverpool against Aston Villa in 2003.

> Kewell even played his Leeds trial matches under the false name of 'Lawrence Davies' due to the fact that his age and nationality made the move illegal.

to Soccer New South Wales. He had the same balance of traits that almost all prodigious athletes possess: he was popular yet independent, and confident yet painstaking. There was also a touch of luck, because while his Marconi teammate Brett Emerton was also signed only Kewell could make the move due to his father's English heritage. Kewell even played his Leeds trial matches under the false name of 'Lawrence Davies' due to the fact that his age and nationality made the move illegal. New South Wales coach David Lee trained Kewell from 11 years of age to his departure, and said the winger's attitude was all that mattered: 'At that stage it's not so much talent,

Kewell and Tim Cahill celebrate qualifying for the Socceroos' first World Cup in 32 years, in November 2005.

but more their approach to the game,' he told FTBL. 'Harry always accepted things as they were. His left foot wasn't bad, but the rest of his game was pretty ordinary. However, he applied himself to everything we gave him and he picked things up quickly due to his drive to get to the top.'

Kewell developed into a typical English footballer for the period: he spoke with a northerner's accent complete with a rough around the edges Geordie dialect. He married young, to a British soap actress in Las Vegas, and while always shy in front of a camera he began to morph into a heavily marketed role model. He and his wife soon became a favourite of the British tabloids and his face became a fixture on Sky Sports commercials, and a defining relationship with controversial cigar-puffing agent Bernie Mandic began.

At the same time . . . Kewell's football was flourishing at a rate Australia has never witnessed before or since. His decision to join Leeds was crucial, as the team was secure in mid-table and becoming a sensational development club, with Kewell their star asset. He played in a wide variety of positions in the Leeds academy, scoring 17 goals in one season as a left back. By the age

> **Kewell's football was flourishing at a rate Australia has never witnessed before or since.**

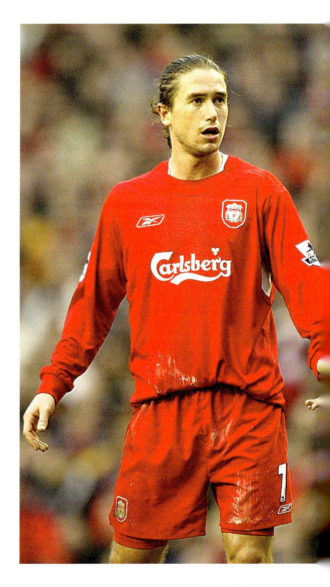

Kewell playing for Liverpool in 2005, the same year he won the Champions League.

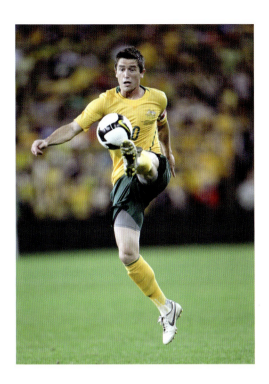

Kewell captained Australia against Iraq in 2008, scoring the only goal in a crucial World Cup qualifier.

of 17 he'd broken into the Leeds first team in time for the club's greatest period under manager David O'Leary: they finished in the Premier League's top five each season and made the semi-finals of the Champions League. Behind the scenes a battle was emerging for Kewell's international allegiance. On the word of English mates, then–Socceroos boss Eddie Thomson sequestered the 17 year old and sent him 10,000 kilometres from Leeds to the Chilean port city of Antofagasta, where he became the third youngest Socceroos debutant in a 3-0 drubbing from the Chileans. 'The pressure on Harry not to play for Australia was huge,' Mandic told FTBL. 'Eddie snuck in under everybody's guard.'

Kewell joined Leeds and the Socceroos at the perfect time. Australia embarked on their longest ever winning streak that year – 14 matches straight – before offering Kewell the ultimate chance to endear himself to the nation. Kewell made just his third Socceroos appearance in the first of a two-legged qualifier for the 1998 World Cup. Two months after his 19th birthday he walked out to a Tehran 'colosseum' in front of a crowd of 128,000 Iranian men hurtling abuse, bottles and even dead chickens at the Australians. He was ready for it, he said later: 'It never really affected me.' In these conditions it only took him 19 minutes to score his first Socceroos goal, which was identical to the one he scored eight years later to send Australia past Croatia: a flick onto his boot, a sumptuous touch and a scorching volley with the opposite foot. The Socceroos escaped Tehran with a 1-1 draw back to the Melbourne Cricket Ground, where in front of 85,000 Australian fans they were expected to reach their first World Cup in 24 years.

Kewell's next appearance was the most devastating day in Australian football history, but it began like any other dream scenario. The flopsy-haired teenager commanded Australia's front line, setting the play before converting a thumping back-post cross to put the Socceroos 1-0 up. He created Australia's second goal as well, but after a lunatic spectator disrupted play Australia conceded two late strikes and a golden generation disappeared on away goals. Just a month later Kewell starred as the Socceroos beat Mexico and drew against Brazil to make the 1997 Confederations Cup semi-final. He scored an incredible long-range strike to win the match against Uruguay, sending Australia to a

Kewell scoring his second goal against Uzbekistan in a 2010 World Cup qualifier.

... 'best left-winger that probably played in England for a long, long time'.

dismal final loss against Brazil. That was Kewell's last Socceroos match for two years. He left West Yorkshire an English lad and returned a hardened Australian veteran; he had been baptised in two cauldrons, shouldering the responsibility of an entire nation. It had taught him that his success depended on himself, not his country.

'He said to me, "Bernie, let me tell you something about football. Mate, you can go beat your wife, beat your kids, root prostitutes, rob a bank or even commit murder – but if you score the winning goal on the weekend, it doesn't fuckin' matter,"' Mandic told *The Sydney Morning Herald*. 'When he said that, I thought, "Fuck me, how cynical can a bloke of 19 be?" But the scary thing was he was right.' Still just 19 years of age, Kewell made 35 appearances for Leeds in 1997/98 in addition to visiting four countries for six Socceroos caps. Next season he made a whopping 49 Leeds appearances and missed every one of Australia's nine matches.

In his fifth season at Leeds, aged just 21, he made an incredible 53 appearances in a single season plus two Australia friendlies.

Kewell averaged a football match every four days for 36 weeks straight, but what made the feat superhuman was that every appearance was a burning intensity of bullet-like speed and implausible dynamism. He was named in the Professional Footballers Association (PFA) Team of the Year and won the PFA Young Player of the Year award, to this date arguably the loftiest individual honour won by an Australian footballer abroad. 'He was one of the reasons I joined Leeds,' Premier League great Rio Ferdinand said. 'He was the star player. His left foot was a wonder at times. He was a bit of a maverick. He scored some unbelievable goals.'

Fellow teammate Ian Harte went even further, calling him the 'best left-winger that probably played in England for a long, long time'. Kewell was nominated for the Ballon d'Or and scored 17 goals that season, forming a prolific partnership with Michael Bridges. 'He could drop the shoulder and be past a player in a flash,' Bridges told *The Guardian*. 'He had that quickness, that skill. I've never had that communication with another striker.' It culminated in a £25 million offer for Kewell from Italian giants Inter Milan, which Leeds rejected. In just six years the windswept blond teen who kicked a ball around for Marconi Stallions in Fairfield had grown from a $2,600 flutter to the most valuable player in the world.

Had Kewell moved to Internazionale that year he would have broken the world transfer record, which in an unbelievable twist of fate had been set by a fellow Marconi Stallions product, Christian Vieri, the previous year. Kewell had created Aussie mania in the Premier League and Leeds rushed to snap up every Australian they could sign; by 2002 he was one of seven Australians at the club and he combined with Mark Viduka for 38 goals that season alone. The next year Kewell destroyed the English national team, as the Socceroos smashed them 3-1 in front of 30,000 fans in London.

At this point the story seems clear – Kewell was a born immortal and Australia was a force majeure – but today these facts are mere trivia. The Socceroos sank to 82nd in the world and five of the seven Aussies at Leeds left within a year. The Australian didn't break the transfer world record; in fact, three years

> **At this point the story seems clear – Kewell was a born immortal and Australia was a force majeure – but today these facts are mere trivia.**

later Leeds collected just £3 million from selling him to Liverpool. Kewell's ticking time bomb had blown. In 2001 he missed 150 days with Achilles tendon problems and, after that, played just one more full season. Bridges hints that century-culminating 2000 season may have been the beginning of the end for Kewell and Leeds' young stars, as the club's utter reliance on the teenagers had placed overwhelming pressure on the young men's bodies: 'Were we told to play as many games, do as many weights as possible?' Bridges asked rhetorically. 'I look back at that team and wonder where it all went wrong. Was it something in our training? We all had success at Leeds, but after that everyone seemed to deteriorate.'

'It's about the mileage that players play,' Kewell's physio, Les Gelis, told FTBL during Kewell's career. 'If you look at the English Premiership in particular, it takes

Kewell playing against Paraguay at Sydney Football Stadium in 2010.

a massive toll on the athlete. If you are a good player, you get played all the time. Harry will never dodge hard work, he is one of the hardest trainers on the pitch . . . his way would be to train all day, every day.'

'An [Achilles] injury stopped him in his tracks,' Ferdinand said. 'He could have gone on to do some magic things.'

There were larger storm clouds on the horizon for Leeds than their treatment of players. Club chairman Peter Risdale had borrowed over $100 million in 2001 against the club's future Champions League revenue. When O'Leary's side narrowly failed to qualify for two consecutive Champions Leagues, Leeds began selling players to finance their debts. After two volatile seasons and with rapid turnover sinking the club to the bottom of the league, Leeds was finally relegated at the end of the 2003/04 season.

Kewell remained with the club until the end, and it's here that the Socceroos' colourful agent Bernie Mandic came into focus. Mandic first struck a relationship with Kewell while he was a Sydney teenager and assisted negotiations for his first Leeds contract. Kewell had grown up a Liverpool fan in Sydney's west, and when Leeds was relegated he rejected bigger-money offers from Barcelona, Real Madrid and Manchester United to play at Anfield. Leeds attempted to block the transfer, but Kewell threatened to sit out his contract and leave for free the following season. Beneath the veil of boyhood dreams, his move reportedly pocketed Mandic nearly as much as Leeds through a private payment, with Liverpool also passing the savings from the low offer onto Kewell's salary. An ensuing war of words played out in the British press, and the resulting controversy followed Kewell for the rest of his Premier League career. It then followed him home, because when an Australian agent issued a complaint over Mandic's transfer Kewell threatened to quit the Socceroos. He may have been able to handle 128,000 Iranians, but playing for one of the world's biggest clubs amid intense media pressure severely rattled him.

Liverpool had huge expectations of Kewell, with manager Gérard Houllier famously passing up the chance to sign Cristiano Ronaldo by saying 'We had Harry Kewell.' His first Liverpool season was very solid, but he wasn't Ronaldo and

Kewell at a fashion shoot at Essendon Airport in 2012, after returning to the A-League amid unprecedented fanfare.

Liverpool weren't title challengers. Then the injuries began: knee, ankle, gout, Achilles, groin, abductor and inguinal hernias, all in addition to autoimmune hepatitis. There were 14 operations, 150 missed club games and 60 missed Socceroos games. 'The bottom of the world is when you are sitting on the edge of the bed crying and wondering "Am I ever going to play the game again?"'

> **1-0 down and believing Kewell was copping out of the contest, they booed him off the pitch.**

he said after winning the Alex Tobin medal. 'You are sitting there going, "What's wrong with me? Every time I am kicking I am ripping a muscle, every time I am turning I am breaking down."'

Injuries didn't destroy Kewell's Liverpool career, but they cast a shadow so dark that the winger's flashes of brilliance could never escape it. An inconspicuous groin injury that didn't even make the match reports ended up defining his Premier League career. New manager Rafa Benitez didn't understand Kewell's injuries and publicly appeared to doubt the Australian, saying his injury 'changes each day' and that 'one day Harry is okay, and the next he says he is unfit'. It's a particularly cruel irony that Kewell's desperation to return to action convinced both his manager and his fans that he wasn't committed to playing. He rushed back for the 2005 League Cup final but further exacerbated his injury and was withdrawn, before what should have been the greatest moment in his club career – Liverpool's timeless Champions League comeback against AC Milan – became the most ignominious.

Benitez shocked fans by starting Kewell in the final, then forcibly withdrew him after just 23 minutes when Kewell's 'groin snapped'. It was later revealed he had acquired a difficult to diagnose groin deformity called Gilmore's groin and he'd been exacerbating it for months. Even worse, however, were the Liverpool fans themselves: 1-0 down and believing Kewell was copping out of the contest, they booed him off the pitch. Consoled by John Arne Riise as he walked off the ground, Kewell stared at the pitch and did his best to keep a straight face, but he admits now it was a 'nightmare'. While his teammates celebrated one of the greatest wins in the club's history he returned to his hotel room, to 'nothing'. The 2006 FA Cup final was the same story, with him starting the match only to be forced off in the 48th minute with an abdominal strain to watch another stunning Liverpool comeback from the sidelines.

The dichotomy of Kewell's career is a metaphor for Australian football history, so it was fitting that immediately after Kewell's lowest ebb he entrenched himself into Socceroos immortality. His injury lay-offs for Liverpool had been well publicised, but less clear is how many Socceroos matches he missed due to injury and how many he missed for his club career. The entire time he had been mired in transfer spats and injury crises the Socceroos had continued to slowly build around him and without him. He missed Australia's nail-biting 2001 Confederations Cup campaign and nearly went three years without playing a Socceroos match outside of England. When the Socceroos played England in London in 2003 he reminded Australians what they were missing, single-handedly destroying the Three Lions in a 3-1 win.

At the same time, the Australian pathway Kewell had paved into the Premier League had finally been successfully travailed by most of the Socceroos squad. Australia had never had a squad this prominent in Europe before, but when the Kewell-less Socceroos slumped out of the 2005 Confederations Cup with three straight losses there wasn't anything to suggest this team was any more a golden generation than the 1997 team that preceded it.

By the time the Socceroos swept through Oceania qualifying for their

When the Socceroos played England in London in 2003 he reminded Australians what they were missing, single-handedly destroying the Three Lions in a 3-1 win.

perennial South American World Cup play-off, Australia's greatest player had only played in nine of a possible 60 Socceroos matches since 1997, but Australia was still shocked when Guus Hiddink benched Kewell for the pivotal final play-off in Sydney against Uruguay. Their surprise was short lived, as Hiddink introduced Kewell after just 37 minutes. He set up Bresciano's equaliser, then scored the crucial first spot kick as Australia became the first nation to qualify for a World Cup via a penalty shoot-out. His World Cup performances were electric, building to that defining goal against Croatia, although the promise of his potential to generations of fans was embittered by three decades of near misses.

Australia had thrashed expectations by progressing, but septic arthritis sidelined Kewell

Kewell playing for Melbourne Victory in an A-League derby after returning to Australia.

for the knockout loss against Italy. Although the injury turned out to be serious his loss was devastating, and criticism of his dedication again bubbled to the surface. He responded as Australia's sole highlight from a nightmarish 2007 Asian Cup campaign, and as his Liverpool career fizzled his Socceroos' career ignited. He played for Australia just four times between 1998 and 2005 but had won a whopping 45 caps by the end of 2009. His bit part in Liverpool's 2007 Champions League final loss was his final disappointment before joining Turkish giants Galatasaray, where he was greeted as a hero and soon became one. He scored 20 seconds into his debut to win the Turkish Super Cup, which despite becoming his only trophy in Istanbul signposted three prolific seasons for club and country.

Kewell was crucial in qualifying Australia for the 2010 World Cup through Asia, captaining the side for the first time, but the World Cup itself was a basket case. He was benched entirely for the team's 4-0 opening loss to Germany and had to defend against accusations he had split the Socceroos dressing room – 'They are always having a go at us' – only to be sent off just 24 minutes into their second match against Ghana. He had blocked a Ghanaian shot on his goal line with his bicep, although his arm had been by his side. The decision was highly controversial, and he said the referee 'killed' his World Cup.

He'd always endured horrible luck at major tournaments, but at 32 years of age he played sensationally in his final Socceroos tournament, the 2011 Asian Cup. He scored three goals – including a 118th minute quarter-final winner – and was named one of the tournament's most valuable players as Australia made the final, narrowly losing to Japan. He returned to the A-League that year to great fanfare and played

> Reading through the winners is a reminder of the curse that prodigy lays on a youngster and the talent that injury lays to waste, but the title of the award is an inspiration.

a personally phenomenal season in a poor Melbourne Victory team. He finally ended his career when he was 35 in 2014 at Melbourne Heart.

The year of his retirement a panel of current and former players, administrators and commentators and a poll of more than 15,000 fans bestowed on him the greatest honour of all: 'Australia's greatest ever footballer'. To this day the annual award for Australia's best young footballer is called the Harry Kewell medal. In 13 years only one recipient – Mat Ryan – has gone on to enjoy an elite career. Reading through the winners is a reminder of the curse that prodigy lays on a youngster and the talent that injury lays to waste, but the title of the award is an inspiration: Kewell endured an entire career of horrible luck and horrific injuries yet he still became an immortal among immortals.

National career		
Years	Appearances (B*)	Goals
1994–2009	151 (171)	38

Club career			
Years	Team	Appearances	Goals
1996–2003	Leeds United	181	45
2003–2008	Liverpool	93	12
2008–2011	Galatasaray SK	63	22
2011–2012	Melbourne Victory	25	8
2012–2013	Al Gharafa	3	1
2013–2014	Melbourne Heart	16	2

Honours	
Confederations Cup All Star	1997
Oceania Footballer of the Year	1999, 2001, 2003
Professional Footballers Association Young Player of the Year	2000
Leeds United Player of the Year	2000
Professional Footballers Association Team of the Year	2000
Ballon d'Or nominee	2001
Asian Cup Team of the Tournament	2007, 2011
Australia's Greatest Ever Footballer	2012
Australia's Greatest Team	2012
Asian Football Hall of Fame	2014
Alex Tobin Medal	2016
Order of Australia	2016
Sport Australia Hall of Fame	2018
Football Federation Australia Hall of Fame	2019

* *Total caps including exhibition, friendlies and other (B) games.*

Tim Cahill's flag-punching celebration is just one of the Australian's global legacies.

Birthdate	6 December 1979
Place of birth	Sydney, New South Wales
Major teams	Australia, Millwall, Everton, New York Red Bulls, Melbourne City
Position	Forward, winger, midfielder

Tim Cahill is the greatest Socceroo of all time and remains the figurehead of Australian men's football. His impact was so widespread for so long the Socceroos may never replace him.

He shot a quick left jab to the stem, a jolting right cross and another left then clutched both fists to his forehead. Chin locked to chest, he powered through the one-two-one before a swift duck and weave and a thumping right hook. The corner flag hit the deck harder than a heavyweight slams the canvas.

The immortal celebration's apt for Australian football's greatest fighter. At a quarter to five in the afternoon in Kaiserslautern a looping throw-in sends yellow and blue shirts scrambling, and in the midst of it all Tim Cahill floats like a butterfly and stings like a bee. His flawless (read: freakish) positional sense stems from the coolest head on the pitch. However, when he hit that winner against the Japanese and as he wagged his fingers at his teammates and the world's cameras focused on his face, there's a fraction of a second when Cahill had to fight back the tears. For the briefest moment his eyes squeezed shut and his mouth trembled as he realised the momentous nature of what he'd achieved: it's a rare glimpse behind the bullish façade into the true heart of the Socceroos' greatest player. By the time his Socceroos teammates piled around him he was already shouting and swearing – testosterone pumping out of every pore – as Australia lived to fight another day.

When Cahill knocked out the flag in the 2006 World Cup, Australian football found its talisman. He scored the Socceroos' first and second World Cup goal on 12 June 2006, and after that the records kept tumbling: he eventually set nearly every Australian milestone and changed the sport forever. He was a legendary figure for English clubs Millwall and Everton, but from this moment until the day he retired he was the face of Australian football across the world. He's Australia's all-time leading male goalscorer. He scored five World Cup goals across four World Cups, an Australian record. He was the first

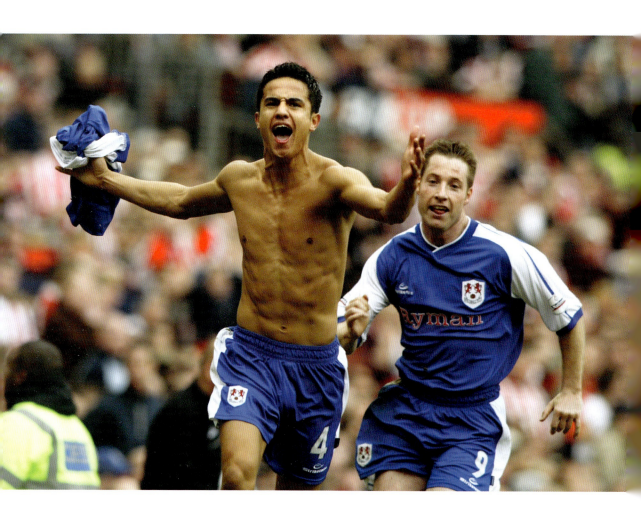

Cahill celebrates scoring the winner against Sunderland to send Millwall into the FA Cup final and UEFA Cup.

> 'I was told I was too small. I was told I wasn't fast enough . . . It was probably the best thing that ever happened to me . . .'

Australian man to score at an Asian Cup and also Australia's highest goal scorer at that tournament. A Ballon d'Or and Puskás Award nominee, Cahill was named Oceania Footballer of the Year just months after his Socceroos debut and Professional Footballers Association (PFA) Player of the Year four years later in 2009, won the Asian Cup seven years after that and became Australia's oldest ever goal scorer another two years later. His 108 Socceroos caps are a record for an outfielder, while his exactly 600 professional league matches and 150 league goals are the tidy bow on the gift that kept giving.

Timothy Filiga Cahill was born in Balmain, Sydney to a proud, sprawling Samoan family that would regularly return to the Polynesian archipelago to visit the remote village where his grandfather was chief. 'We would wake up at five in the morning and go to get the hot bread and then go back home to eat it with butter, maybe with eggs if they were available,' he told the *Daily Mail*. 'Then we went to the shower, which was the watering hole across the road. Life was very simple.' There are no less than nine family members who've played either league or union professionally. 'Basically, if you give me a rugby ball I can juggle it,' he says.

In contrast to the Samoan heritage he has inked around his arm, his father, Tim Cahill senior, was an oil rigger and trawler from Dagenham. He travelled the world as a merchant seaman, occasionally training with South American clubs in the 1960s. He was infatuated with football, so when he suffered a work injury during Cahill's youth he focused on training his three sons, taking them to local parks and forcing them to play without right boots to develop their left feet: training that would eventually create one of the World Cup's greatest goals 30 years later. 'As a boy, I used to see the lights flickering in the hallway in the early hours and know my dad was watching the football on TV,' Cahill told The Father Hood. 'I'd sneak out of my bedroom and hide behind the settee to watch too. Dad would let me watch for a while; Serie A or Premier League highlights. Then he'd send me back to bed.'

Cahill attended four different schools and played for three different football clubs around the Sydney area before playing in the youth teams for National Soccer League (NSL) clubs Sydney Olympic and Sydney United between 1995 and 1997. The clubs were sceptical of Cahill's ability: he was a short and slight child who was repeatedly told he could never amount to being a professional footballer. 'I was told I was too small. I was told I wasn't fast enough,' Cahill told *The Sydney Morning Herald* (*SMH*). 'It was probably the best thing that ever happened to me, being told I would never be a professional football player.'

While he now credits his doubters with entrenching his determination, Australia's scepticism nearly cost the Socceroos' Cahill altogether. Both he and his older brother Sean represented Samoa at youth level, and his younger brother Chris went on to captain the Samoan national team. The Samoan Football Federation invited 14-year-old Cahill to join Sean at a national U/20 training camp and was amazed at the boy's ability. Five years younger than anyone else on the park, he played for Samoa's U/20 side in two official FIFA matches against New Zealand and Vanuatu in 1994. For Cahill, the tournament was merely a chance to visit his

Cahill's Socceroos portrait before the 2006 World Cup.

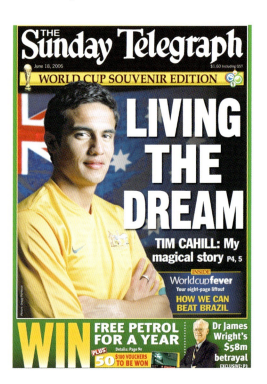

Cahill became Australian football's posterboy after scoring the Socceroos' first and second World Cup goals.

> 'I used to cry on the phone all the time . . . I was living in digs with a family I'd never met before – a kid on the other side of the world; lights off and you're alone – that's the reality.'

sick grandmother on the Samoan federation's expense. Unbeknown to him, it made him ineligible to play for Australia.

By 1997 at the age of 16, Cahill was adamant he could skip the NSL altogether and go directly to Europe. His father had an old contact at Millwall that would give him a trial, but his parents had to take out a $30,000 loan to send him to England on a family exchange program. His father's unrequited football love encouraged him to take a huge risk on his second born but this also impacted the future careers of Cahill's brothers, who had to begin working to finance the family's debt. 'I used to cry on the phone all the time,' Cahill told the *SMH*. 'I was living in digs with a family I'd never met before – a kid on the other side of the world; lights off and you're alone – that's the reality.'

Cahill's family's belief paid off where Australia's hadn't, as he quickly earned a youth contract with Millwall and never looked back. The determination he'd fostered to survive abroad enabled him to survive the fans and dressing room at England's toughest club. He excelled for the next seven seasons, but his familial ties kept him grounded. 'I was signing my first contract at Millwall and I wanted to buy myself a nice new car,' he told The Father Hood. 'You can't live in a car,' his father responded. 'After talking it over, instead I invested that signing-on fee with my family. We all saved up – my parents, my brother and myself. Together we bought our first home in Horningsea Park, in the outer west of Sydney.'

Cahill made his Millwall debut aged 18 in 1998 and was catapulted into their first team the next season for one of the proudest periods in Millwall's history. They made the Football League Trophy Final in 1999, losing to Wigan Athletic, then went on to win the Second Division in 2000/01 with a club record of 93 points. Cahill then anchored Millwall's midfield – scoring three goals, including the winner in the semi-final at Sunderland – as the Lions made the FA Cup final in

Tim Cahill · 101

2004 against Manchester United at Wembley and qualified for the UEFA Cup.

At first glance Cahill was a solid all-rounder at The Den without technical excellence or physical superiority, yet beneath the surface was a ferocious and intelligent box-to-box midfielder with tactical nous and a work ethic to match. He had a unique array of what football coaches call 'one-per centers' that enabled him to become a unique world-class footballer and a knack for reading attacking play and finding the perfect position in the goal mouth, which made him a surprisingly prolific goal scorer. However, his ultimate defiant characteristic, directed squarely at the naysayers who called him too small, was the greatest vertical leap the world has ever seen.

Cahill's two English nicknames, 'Tiny Tim' and the 'Blue Kangaroo', tell the story. For his entire career he

> **For his entire career he was the greatest header of the ball per inch in the world, scoring 31 of his 56 career Premier League goals with his head.**

Cahill, deadliest from headers and volleys, hits a scissor kick against Oman in 2013.

Cahill captaining the Socceroos against South Africa in the lead-up to the 2014 World Cup.

was the greatest header of the ball per inch in the world, scoring 31 of his 56 career Premier League goals with his head. 'Before every game, my analysis was important,' he told the Premier League. 'You never saw me go near post, because it would more than likely go over my head. I wanted to know who the weakest centre-back was, and who could turn off his left shoulder better than his right.'

Cahill developed his world-leading attacking expertise by playing 250 professional games and scoring a whopping 57 goals by the time he was 25. He scored 12 goals in 45 league matches in his second Millwall season, then 13 in 43 matches in 2001/02. It was enough to grab the attention of both the Irish (through his father's heritage) and Australian national teams but Cahill, who 'couldn't care less about playing' for Samoa, was cap tied and ineligible for either. Staring down an anonymous Oceanian future, he threatened to sue FIFA for the right to change his eligibility. Luckily for him the organisation changed its rules the following year, allowing him to represent another nation. Australia wasn't about to make the same mistake twice: after he scored three times in four Olyroos appearances in 2004 he was thrown straight into the Socceroos' line-up.

This was the beginning of an epic year for the Australian icon. It began with a £1.5 million move

Thirty-five-year-old Cahill scored three goals in the 2015 Asian Cup to lead the Socceroos to the title.

to Everton – later labelled one of the bargains of the century – and ended with Cahill scoring six times as the Socceroos won the 2004 Oceania Football Confederation Nations Cup, finishing the year with seven goals in his first five Australian caps. He married his childhood sweetheart and his first son Kyah was born that year. Then just 24 years of age, Cahill called it a shock: Kyah had non-stop colic for the first year 'so we didn't get much sleep'. Most distressingly, his older brother Sean, whom Cahill had followed into football, partially blinded a man in a street brawl in London and fled to Sydney for two years before being extradited and jailed in 2006.

Cahill's chaotic personal life was exacerbated by a huge increase in pressure, as he'd been thrown from the sodden pitches of England's second tier to the glitz and glamour of the Premier League, which was rapidly becoming the richest league in the world. He was brought into a bloated and ageing Everton squad under David Moyes, who was focusing on a long-term transition towards developing younger talent. It proved the perfect move for Cahill, who later said he had to be an 'eight or nine' in every training session while his teammates only had to be 'sixes'. He excelled against the odds, winning Everton's golden boot with 11 goals in 33 appearances in his debut season. It would prove to be the Toffees legend's most prolific campaign: he won Oceania Footballer of the Year, PFA Team of the Year, Everton Player of the Year and Players' Player of the Season honours that season. By 25 Cahill had finally arrived, and he was making up for lost time.

He became a Socceroos regular at the 2005 Confederations Cup, then endeared himself to Guus Hiddink by playing sensationally in Sydney as Australia beat Uruguay on penalties to qualify for the 2006 World Cup. He wrote his name into Australian sporting folklore at that tournament against Japan, playing every subsequent match.

The Socceroos played their debut Asian Cup campaign in Thailand the following year. Cahill was recovering from an injury, and an over-confident and underprepared squad was one minute away from an embarrassing opening loss to Oman before he came off the bench to once again score Australia's first goal at a major tournament, rescuing his country when they needed him most.

He affirmed his big-game reputation for Everton, becoming their first player since the 1930s to score in three Merseyside Derbies. To this day he's Everton's highest goal scorer against Liverpool since World War Two. He first captained Everton in 2009, leading the side to his second FA Cup final, and scored his 50th Toffees goal by 2010. He played 278 matches for Everton, scoring 68 goals in all competitions despite injuries hampering the most prolific period of his career: between 2006 and

Cahill chasing down the ball in the 2015 Asian Cup final against South Korea.

Cahill attempting a bicycle kick for Melbourne City after returning to the A-League in 2016.

2008. It was obvious to many that Cahill could be an incredible striker, however, it took until the twilight years of his career before a coach eventually used him to devastating goal-scoring effect.

Cahill's phenomenal Socceroos performances in World Cup and Asian Cup qualifiers entrenched his reputation as a national saving grace. By 2010 he'd scored 21 goals in 35 Socceroos games, leading Rale Rasic to say to *The Australian*: 'Without a doubt, [he is] the best Australian footballer I have seen. He is the complete footballer. He has presence, poise and the ability to read the game. He is great in the air, his heading is exceptional. He is an extraordinary goal-scorer and he just knows where to be at the right time. You can't coach that in a player. You are born with it. It's pure natural ability.'

After his heroics in 2006, Cahill's 2010 World Cup campaign was nearly over before it began. He was sent off in Australia's first match for a tackle on German midfielder Bastian Schweinsteiger, who was so insistent the red card was undeserved that he signed a document calling for leniency. Cahill was then suspended for Australia's second game but wouldn't be denied a dying World Cup impact nonetheless, returning in Australia's final match to score a perfect glancing header against Serbia to ensure the Socceroos departed with a win.

> **He scored a ridiculous 19 goals in 28 Socceroos caps from the ages of 34 to 36.**

While Harry Kewell and Mark Viduka failed to fulfil their momentous Socceroos expectations, Cahill's surprise prolificacy for club and country gave him superstar status, which he relished after leaving Everton in 2012. By then 32 years of age, he moved to Major League Soccer (MLS) to sign for New York Red Bulls, an Australian teaching the Americans how to play a European game. After a slow start he exploded in his second season, scoring 11 goals in 27 appearances and winning the Bulls' most valued player and golden boot awards, plus MLS XI selection the following year. He even set the MLS record for the league's fastest ever goal, striking a long-range effort against Houston just seven seconds after kick-off.

By the 2014 World Cup the rest of the golden generation had retired, cementing Cahill as not only Australian football's unrivalled poster boy but it's only attacking weapon. A reborn striker at 34, he scored at his third successive World Cup in Australia's first match against Chile. In their second game against the Dutch he made every newsreel and back page around the world, scoring a blinding, first-touch, left-footed volley from a 30 metre long ball. The greatest World Cup goal scorer of all time, Ronaldo, told FIFA: 'It was the best goal of the World Cup and it's going to go down in history as one of the most beautiful World Cup goals.'

When he was 35 Cahill scored three goals at the 2015 Asian Cup, including a bicycle-cum-scissor kick against China in the semi-final, to lead Australia to their first major international trophy. He scored a ridiculous 19 goals in 28 Socceroos caps from the ages of 34 to 36. He'd cashed in on his evergreen status in 2014, signing a $10 million deal with Chinese club Shanghai Shenhua, but insinuated later that the weight of his pay packet and superstar status put too much pressure on his goal tally. He was a player who was always better flying under the radar, which would never be possible again.

In 1997 Cahill escaped a dissolving, semi-professional wilderness with few fans and fewer prospects as a shy, written-off teenager. He returned 20 years later as arguably the most famous Australian athlete of all time and joined a Melbourne club with owners worth trillions of

Tim Cahill · 107

Cahill celebrates his final Socceroos goal, his 50th in 103 caps, against Syria in 2017.

dollars, to score a 40 metre volley against Melbourne Victory in front of 50,000 packed fans in one of the highest-profile sporting leagues in Asia. Nobody has transformed the Australian sporting landscape more than he has, achieving so much for so many from so little. He played in his fifth World Cup campaign in 2018 before making his 108th and final Socceroos appearance against Lebanon, waving goodbye to a capacity Australian home crowd.

Cahill is only one year younger than the man voted 'Australia's Greatest Ever Footballer', Harry Kewell, but had to wait eight years longer to make his Australian debut, yet he still made 50 more appearances and scored 33 more goals in green and gold. He exceeded his potential by so much it overshadowed two generations of Australians who didn't. What's most remarkable is that his achievements for the Socceroos were embraced by the entire world and continue to resonate on the world stage to this day.

'Think about it,' the now-analyst and coach told Red Bull. 'You can have an impact on the park. You can score those goals, you can create amazing moments, but you think people will forget you. You don't realise . . . Then I go back to England and I'm sitting on the panel of Sky Sports and Match of the Day, and then you're like, "I've been away for eight years, and still now I'm getting stopped." You then realise what an impact you actually made to the game. It's the best feeling ever.'

National career		
Years	Appearances	Goals
2004–2018	108	50

Club career			
Years	Team	Appearances	Goals
1997–2004	Millwall	250	57
2004–2012	Everton	278	68
2012–2014	New York Red Bulls	72	16
2015	Shanghai Shenhua	28	11
2016	Hangzhou Greentown	17	4
2016–2018	Melbourne City	34	13
2017–2018	Millwall	10	0
2018–2019	Jamshedpur	12	2

Honours	
Oceania Football Confederation Nations Cup	2004
Professional Footballers Association First Division Team of the Year	2004
Oceania Footballer of the Year	2004
Everton Golden Boot	2004
FA Cup runner-up	2004, 2009
Everton Player of the Season	2005
Everton Players' Player of the Season	2005
Ballon d'Or nominee	2006
Professional Footballers Association Player of the Year	2009
Australia's Greatest Team	2012
Major League Soccer Supporters' Shield	2013
New York Red Bulls Golden Boot	2013
Major League Soccer Best XI	2013
New York Red Bulls Most Valuable Player	2013
Asian Football Hall of Fame	2014
Puskás Award nominee	2014
Asian Cup	2015
Asian Cup Team and Goal of Tournament	2015
Football Federation Australia Cup	2016
Asian Football Confederation Asian Icon	2017
Asian Football Confederation All-Time World Cup XI	2020
Order of Australia	2021

Lisa De Vanna showcases her amazing dribbling skills, arguably the best in Australian football, against Chile in 2018.

LISA DE VANNA

Birthdate	14 November 1984
Place of birth	Perth, Western Australia
Major teams	Australia, Brisbane Roar, Melbourne Victory, Melbourne City, Fiorentina
Position	Forward, winger

> Lisa De Vanna stormed the Matildas into the modern era. She was an enigmatic virtuoso who stylistically transformed her national team and became one of the most influential footballers in Australian history.

It was the Matildas' first trophy in 10 years but it was also their third match that week. It was hot and it was late; they were 13,000 kilometres from home and everyone in the Californian crowd was rooting against the underdog. They were facing a football monolith – spearheaded by the greatest female footballer of all time – and within two minutes they were 1-0 down. To top it all off, Lisa De Vanna, with black armband pulled high, had stepped up to the spot and her shot was saved.

Nothing De Vanna has ever achieved came easily. The few goalkeepers lucky enough to save a De Vanna shot soon found out that unless they clutch the ball tighter than a tourniquet she'd kick off an arm to get it into the back of the net. The pint-sized 32 year old smashed home the rebound. Game on. Before anyone could catch their breath she burst through again to assist the second. Of course she was offside, but by then it didn't matter. When De Vanna flicked the switch it's not a matter of if, but when. The favourites tried to steady themselves, so De Vanna scored again. Her second goal was her 41st in green and gold, but this time she flung her arms wide and threw her head back towards the sky before squeezing Sam Kerr tight. Turning, she ran to the touchline and jumped into the arms of the Matildas' applauding coaching staff.

De Vanna lines up for the Matildas in 2013 against China.

At full time the global headlines read: 'Australia 6-1 Brazil'.

For seven glorious days in 2017 Australia had the greatest football team on the planet. On Thursday night they'd coolly dispatched reigning World Cup winners USA on their own home turf, and on Sunday around lunchtime they'd thumped four goals past World Cup runners-up Japan. Finally, on a Wednesday afternoon the Matildas achieved the most gobsmacking result in Australian football history. When De Vanna stepped onto that field in Carson she was no longer the Matildas' biggest star. That honour – for which she'd had to overcome insurmountable odds – had been usurped by Kerr, the team's epically talented, perfectly photogenic, back-flipping golden girl. Kerr epitomised the modern, fashionable Matildas while De Vanna was a pugnacious gas station clerk who fought teammates and swore like a trooper. But while Kerr is the hero Australian football needed, De Vanna was the one it deserved. The Matildas dismantled Brazil two days after the death of football icon Les Murray, who dedicated his life to seeing Australia achieve results like these.

De Vanna, more than any other Matilda, encapsulated that struggle for recognition. 'Today was emotional,' she told AAP post match. 'Les was a pioneer. He was like us women, fighting to show what we can do, and for Australia.'

De Vanna evolved Australian football more than any other player, and her tribute to its past was apt at its latest peak. Her 41st goal that day made her the highest goal scorer in Matildas history at the time, and she finished her career with 47 goals in 150 Matildas appearances. Until her final years she was the most brilliant footballer the Matildas had ever seen, radically re-evaluating the way a Matildas side could play, yet crucially she still encapsulated the working-class grit and thuggish determination that defined the Matildas' journey to football's pinnacle. No other figure better defines the Matildas.

Born in a multicultural pocket of Fremantle to a Portuguese mother and Italian father, De Vanna

De Vanna's success is largely due to her formidable combination of pace, balance and ball control.

De Vanna showcases her goal-scoring versatility, with her 31st career goal against China.

inherited a fiery personality and an 'unhealthy obsession' with football. Her brother is 10 years older, but she insisted on playing street football with him and the neighbourhood boys of a day, and at night she slept with a football in her bed. Asthmatic and only 156 centimetres tall as an adult, as a child she was outmatched in every way but it was her 'ruthless' brother who forged her steely resolve: he never let her win and demanded she get up any time she cried.

'My brother was very rough,' she told ESPN. 'That's the way I play.'

She was a prodigy who could juggle by six years of age, but with no Women's National Soccer League (WSNL) team in Western Australia she dominated inter-school competitions. She came from a poor background and her upbringing was tough, so by her teenage years she was storming out of classrooms and her friends were using drugs. Yet football had become a powerful raison d'être – a self-described 'addiction' – and it controlled her life. She dedicated herself to the round ball long before she knew the Matildas existed, and at 14 years of age it steered her out of Fremantle to a tournament in New South Wales, where by either destiny or dumb luck the only other Australian woman in history with De Vanna's dedication was watching. Cheryl Salisbury observed an emphatic De Vanna win the same most valued player award she had won many years earlier. The Matildas icon walked over, wrapped an arm around De Vanna and said: 'I've seen you play. You will play for the Matildas one day.'

'From that day on I made it my goal to play for the Matildas,' De Vanna told My Football. 'I'd do whatever it took to get there.'

De Vanna sold raffle tickets and relied on her mother's Centrelink payments to pay for her first training camp at the Australian Institute of Sport. They instantly noticed her talent, but the nearest WNSL side was thousands of kilometres away in Adelaide. At the age of 15 she left home alone, deserting school and surviving on the dole and living with coaches or much older teammates just for a chance to be noticed. She had to pay to play for her WNSL side, and even if she made the Matildas it would be unpaid. The incredible risk she took as an adolescent seems like madness, but it quickly became clear to anyone watching that she could change Australian football forever.

At 16, in her first year playing against toughened senior women, De Vanna won the league's best player – the Julie Dolan Medal – and the golden boot. She was expected to star at FIFA's first women's youth tournament, the 2002 U/19 World Championship, but she was kicked off the Australian team for her wild behaviour and selfish play. That tournament kick-started professional careers for the world's greatest female footballers, from Brazil's six-time FIFA World Player of the Year Marta to the world's highest international goal scorer, Canada's Christine Sinclair. However, De Vanna's hapless suspension stagnated her prodigious talent, miring her in amateur Australian competitions for another four years. To any other homesick teenager this could have been the killer blow, but for De Vanna it was just another roadblock. She told SBS: 'I always knew it was going to happen, it was just a matter of when.'

In 2004 the WNSL collapsed, throwing many Matildas' futures into jeopardy, but De Vanna excelled in the midst of football's chaos. She and Sarah Walsh debuted for the Matildas on the same day, forming a dynamic attack that transformed the national team. De Vanna was a revelation, scoring a brace in her second game and Australia's only goal against world champions China in her third. Her low centre of gravity amplified her speed and trickery and her left footedness – like Marta, Diego Maradona and Lionel Messi – made her especially unpredictable. The amateur Matildas had never had a player as unstoppable as she was and she instantly changed the team's tactical approach, re-evaluating how an Australian side could play. The teenager was catapulted from park football to play across Fiji, China, Mexico and the USA. In August her sacrifices truly paid off, when the dole-bludging rebel became an Olympian at the 2004 Athens Olympic Games.

She entered the Matildas' first match in the 57th minute against Brazil and her live-wire performance nearly created three goals in front of 25,000 fans. She was equally dominant in their second game against hosts Greece, and had a goal controversially disallowed as the Matildas secured their first Olympic

'The people that don't know me don't. I get told this a million times, that you are the most misunderstood person I have ever met.'

victory. Their third match was against the world's greatest team, the United States. Australia was losing but De Vanna's introduction changed the game again, creating the equaliser that sent the Matildas to the quarter-finals. She was constantly played off the bench – Craig Foster wrote that 'she runs on jet fuel, which burns twice as fast' – but the Matildas still relied heavily on her. In the quarters Sweden scored twice early and she was introduced after just 37 minutes, immediately beating two defenders to nearly assist Walsh. After half-time she latched on to a lose midfield ball, tore past her marker and slotted a low effort past the onrushing goalkeeper for her first Olympic goal. Australia lost 2-1, but in her first six months De Vanna had led the Matildas to their first major tournament victory and quarter-final, as well as their first positive result in 16 attempts against the USA.

In 2006 Australia hosted the Asian Cup – almost entirely at

De Vanna at the 2016 Dolan Warren Awards, 13 years after she won the Julie Dolan medal.

Adelaide's Hindmarsh Stadium – in the country's first tournament in the Asian confederation. Sparse media and an apathetic public welcomed the Matildas but De Vanna was burning with ambition, scoring in each of their first three matches. They comfortably beat heavyweights South Korea and Japan to make their first major tournament final against China, only to blow a 2-0 lead in regular time and miss two penalties in the resulting shoot-out. Their rapid succession signalled the Matildas could be a global force, but their ultimate collapse also hinted at fragility within the squad. The Matildas stormed through qualifying for the Beijing Olympics in 2007, scoring a ridiculous 45 goals in five matches, but once again fell at the final hurdle. An over-confident team faced North Korea in a two-legged play-off and lost both legs listlessly.

De Vanna once told *The Sydney Morning Herald*: 'The people that don't know me don't. I get told this a million times, that you are the most misunderstood person I have ever met.' This is at least partly because she's a person of immense contradictions. SBS' Lucy Zelić wrote after meeting De Vanna that what she first thought was nervousness was actually 'passion in its purest form'. The first thing you notice about De Vanna is her enveloping, wide-set grin, with all the warmth of an Italian nonna. Behind the embracing demeanour is a self-described 'psycho', a merciless competitor and teammate who is quick to argue, criticise and complain and never suffers fools. Her diminutive stature and naturally stocky build belies her incredible speed and agility, and by the age of 23 she was the fastest player in women's football.

De Vanna epitomised the ambition of a new generation of female athletes, but her outspoken persona clashed in a crucible of different aspirations, experiences, lifestyles and sexualities in the Matildas. Many of her teammates were juggling careers and families and had no promise of professionalism on the horizon. In contrast, De Vanna longed to be one of the world's greatest footballers and moved to Europe to play in fledgling semi-professional leagues in England and Sweden. She wrote for Players Voice that while the Matildas had a 'great core' they were a 'team of thugs that just kicked players'.

'In the past [other Matildas] didn't care – but I cared,' she told *The Guardian*. 'So then I'm the one blowing up because I wanted the best for myself, I wanted the best for my team and I expected better from my teammates.' Matildas coach Tom Sermanni told *The Sydney Morning Herald*: 'She's not difficult in the sense that she's a prima donna. Nor does she cause unrest by being disruptive in a team sense. But she puts herself under so much pressure. And the more the pressure builds up, she feels it and I liken her to a pressure cooker, she suddenly explodes.' Her long-term Western Australian coach Alistair Edwards was less diplomatic in 2007, calling her 'brilliant' and a 'brat'. 'I give shit

De Vanna played for Fiorentina in Italy in 2020, in a new era for female football at major European clubs.

to everyone,' De Vanna wrote. 'I stir things up.'

In the Matildas' first match of the 2007 World Cup De Vanna scored a brace off the bench in a 4-1 win, toying with her tiring Ghanaian opponents in 30 degree heat to earn the Matildas their first World Cup victory. She backed that up by scoring the Matildas' greatest World Cup goal against world number four Norway. Alone, she sprinted directly at three central defenders, darting right then left at the final second and sending two sprawling on the turf. At full stretch she didn't even

> **Her father had died three months before the tournament, and as she grounded herself on the world stage she gazed upwards, pointing at the sky.**

glance at the goal before firing into the top corner from well outside the box. Australia needed a draw against Canada in their final group match and were 2-1 down in the 92nd minute, only for De Vanna to shimmy and sidestep through two Canadian defenders in a packed penalty area before forcing the ball to Salisbury to score the equaliser.

The Matildas faced rivals Brazil in the quarters and lost 3-2, but De Vanna scored a brilliant solo goal again. Her father had died three months before the tournament, and as she grounded herself on the world stage she gazed upwards, pointing at the sky. She was nominated for FIFA World Player of the Year and named in FIFA's World Cup All Star team. Her performances captured the Australian public's attention for the first time, and the next year female football participation rose by 10 per cent. From that tournament on no amount of controversy could ever overshadow her pure footballing genius.

The A-League Women was founded in 2008 on the back of the Matildas' success, beginning a new era for women's football. The competition ran during summer and the USA's new league ran in winter, so De Vanna became one of the first Matildas to play club football all year round. It wasn't full professionalism; she returned from the World Cup to a job at a Shell petrol station and would lie to customers who asked if she was 'that soccer player', but it allowed her to face the world's best footballers for up to six months per year, entrenching the high standards she expected from herself and others. It transformed her training regime and at 24 years of age she hit her physical peak, transitioning from an impact substitute to a 90 minute stalwart for the national team just before a horrific injury foreshadowed her darkest year.

Australia entered the 2010 Asian Cup brimming with confidence and won both opening matches, making their third a dead rubber. De Vanna was supposed to be rested, but after the Matildas conceded early Sermanni couldn't resist her potential impact. Within minutes of her introduction her leg struck China's onrushing goalkeeper at full stretch, snapping her foot backwards, breaking her leg and damaging her ankle ligaments. She didn't believe the extent of the injury afterwards, arguing with her team's doctors from fear she would never return the same player. From the team's hotel in China she watched the Matildas win their first major tournament without her, but rather than experiencing it as a bittersweet moment she was elated, refusing to take painkillers so she could feel her teammates' emotions. She had spent her entire career valuing the Matildas over herself, watching their matches unfold from the dugout and knowing that the difference between a win and loss was her introduction at the perfect time.

When De Vanna was nearing the end of her recovery six months later a media storm literally added insult to injury when a young fan found sexually explicit images on her Facebook page. The tabloid scorn was humiliating and her career hit its nadir on her return to the national team in 2011, when she was expelled from a Matildas camp for refusing to meet media commitments. However, while it was constantly stretched, the bond between De Vanna, her teammates and her

'I never thought that anyone would ever consider seeing me as a leader.'

coaches never broke. She rebounded excellently just three weeks later, scoring, assisting and playing in all four matches as the Matildas made their second successive World Cup quarter-final. She had a less demonstrative impact as a starting player in a team that no longer required her to single-handedly grab games by the throat for better or worse. Sermanni was also intent on evolving the squad and introducing the Matildas' next generation. With 13 players under 23, the Matildas failed to qualify for their second straight Olympics in 2012. It appeared they'd reached their limit, and Sermanni left the role.

While her national career had been limited, De Vanna expressed her full individuality for her clubs. She scored the winner in the 2011 A-League Women grand final for her first championship with Brisbane Roar. In 2013, the same year she won Football Federation Australia's Female Footballer of the Year, her agility went viral around the world when she scored a perfect bicycle kick in the USA that was nominated for FIFA's Puskás Award. She scored in the 2014 A-League Women grand final to win her second championship with Melbourne Victory, but before the 2015 World Cup a reflective De Vanna believed her career was coming to an end. The Matildas had appointed as their new coach Alen Stajcic, who had previously scorned De Vanna for a brutal challenge on fellow Matildas star Elyse Perry. Instead, Stajcic made the inspired decision to name her Matildas co-captain. She cried when he told her, telling SBS: 'I never thought that anyone would ever consider seeing me as a leader.'

De Vanna captained the Matildas for her 100th cap, in the first match of the 2015 World Cup against the USA, and scored to mark the occasion. She dribbled past three opponents to assist Simon's winner against Nigeria in the second match then scored a beautiful goal after just five minutes to secure a draw against Sweden in their third. In the next round, facing the insurmountable Brazil, a powerful De Vanna shot allowed Australia to score from the rebound and they held on for the

De Vanna playing for Fiorentina against Roma in 2020.

country's first knockout win at a World Cup. Her leadership pushed a Matildas squad with an average age of just 23 further than the men's or women's national teams had been before. Eight years after her first award and aged 31 she once again made FIFA's All Star team.

De Vanna was uncompromising, refusing to strike alongside her own players for better conditions, but she was also a natural leader. In 2016 she captained Melbourne City to the greatest campaign in A-League Women history, winning all 12 matches and scoring in her third grand final for her third championship. She then led the Matildas to break their Olympic drought for Rio de Janeiro in 2016, spearheading them to the quarter-finals of a major tournament for the fifth time and scoring in her ninth major tournament. When she became their highest goal scorer at the Tournament of Nations the Matildas also cemented themselves as global superstars: they were ranked fourth in the world, won polls for Australia's favourite sporting team and began to sell out every home fixture. At 34 De Vanna continued to lead the side despite the plethora of young talent, playing in 15 of the Matildas' 17 matches in 2018 and leading Australia

In 2004 De Vanna started her debut Matildas match, unpaid, in front of empty stands at a quiet Brisbane athletics field for a team most Australians had never heard of.

to her fifth Asian Cup and fourth final. At the age of 37 she continued to devastate defences, winning the 2021 A-League Women Goal of the Year for an incredible solo run.

In 2004 De Vanna started her debut Matildas match, unpaid, in front of empty stands at a quiet Brisbane athletics field for a team most Australians had never heard of. Fifteen years later she started in her final Matildas match at the 2019 World Cup in front of tens of millions of viewers across the globe, paid equally to her Socceroos counterparts, for one of the world's greatest famous teams. She was asked later if she wanted a testimonial match, which would have seen her equal Salisbury's all-time Australian appearance record. De Vanna's response was like her – short and barely sweet: 'No way, no platitudes.' Perhaps that's her greatest legacy after all.

National career		
Years	Appearances	Goals
2004–2019	150	47

Club career*			
Years	Team	Appearances	Goals
2001–2004	Adelaide Sensation	–	–
2004–2008	Western Waves	–	–
2006–2007	Doncaster Belles	–	–
2008–2009	AIK Fotboll	19	15
2008–2009	Perth Glory	8	2
2009–2010	Washington Freedom	21	7
2010–2011	Brisbane Roar	9	4
2011	Florida MagicJack	8	3
2011–2012	Newcastle Jets	9	5
2012	Linköping	22	7
2012–2013	Perth Glory	7	4
2013	Sky Blue FC	16	5
2013–2015	Melbourne Victory	25	11
2014	Washington Spirit	11	1
2015–2016	Melbourne City	9	3
2016–2017	Canberra United	6	0
2017	South Melbourne	16	18
2017–2019	Sydney FC	24	6
2019–2020	Fiorentina	14	5
2020–2021	Melbourne Victory	12	3

Honours	
Julie Dolan Medal	2003
Women's National Soccer League Golden Boot	2003
FIFA World Cup All Stars	2007, 2015
FIFA Player of the Year nominee	2007
FIFA Puskás Award nominee	2013
FFA Female Footballer of the Year	2013
A-League Women	2011, 2014, 2016, 2019, 2021

* Not all appearances and goals have been recorded.

Craig Johnston is Australia's most successful footballer in Europe. He is pictured here playing for Liverpool in 1986.

9

CRAIG JOHNSTON

Birthdate	25 June 1960
Place of birth	Johannesburg, South Africa
Major teams	Liverpool, Middlesbrough
Position	Midfielder, winger

Craig Johnston is the most successful Australian footballer of all time, and boasts one of the greatest – and strangest – underdog tales in sporting history.

As Craig Johnston teemed down the touchline in the 62nd minute of the 1986 FA Cup final, he couldn't have possibly comprehended the significance of what he was about to accomplish. A native South African raised in Lake Macquarie, he was told his left leg would have to be amputated at the age of six. His parents had sold their house to fund his trial trip to England when he was 15, just for Johnston to be told he was the 'worst footballer' Jack Charlton had 'ever seen in my life'. He lived in a coal shed in Middlesbrough, washing players' cars and boots because he had no money to return home.

Then, 11 years later, he was about to become the first Australian to score in the world's biggest club game for the world's biggest club team and against their biggest rivals. With the scrappiness that defined his career the ball ricocheted through the Everton centre backs and sailed through Kenny Dalglish's legs, but the ever-reliable Johnston slammed it into the back of the net. There was no sound in football as momentous as 98,000 erupting fans at Wembley Stadium. His wild locks abounded as he jumped heroically in the air, scissor kicking his legs beneath him before being swamped by the greatest team England has ever seen. For the first time ever Australia belonged at global football's pinnacle.

Johnston wasn't your average football superstar: physically superhuman but tactically benign, he brought Australia's never say die approach to the world game and succeeded against all odds. He is typically understated; 'I just ran around crazy,' he described as the threat of losing his leg as a child never left him. His narrow escape left a burning desire to outrun and outgun everything in his path. He even looked wild. It was the 1980s and perms were de rigueur, yet his mazy mop of dark curls, burly frame and huge cartoon grin made him the 'he-man' of English football. His accomplishments are unparalleled by any Australian footballer; there's no one who even comes close. Football stories are full of superlatives – everyone's the greatest, every story is rags to riches

Craig Johnston soars through the air in celebration after scoring for Liverpool against Manchester City in 1982.

. . . why isn't Johnston an Australian household name on an altar alongside Tim Cahill and Sam Kerr? As you'll soon find out, nine words were all it took.

– but his career is among the most incredible and unlikely of all time.

The Liverpool side Johnston broke into was arguably the greatest football team of all time, and he played 271 games in just seven years. He won the European Cup, five league titles, an FA Cup, two League Cups and a charity shield. Nicknamed 'Skippy', he was a crowd sensation who ran until he dropped and regularly lost the ball just to turn and chase it down the other end of the pitch like a 'maniac'.

All this from the worst footballer Charlton had ever seen? A near-amputee, a homeless teenager in the Yorkshire winter? It all begs the question: why isn't Johnston an Australian household name on an altar alongside Tim Cahill and Sam Kerr? As you'll soon find out, nine words were all it took.

Craig Peter Johnston was born in Johannesburg in 1960 to Australian parents. His mother Dorothy was a teacher and his father Colin was an amateur footballer with failed dreams. At six years of age Johnston developed the bone infection osteomyelitis, a bacterial disease similar to polio that spreads quickly through the blood and can rot through bone. At the time it happened it could be fatal. The doctors told Johnston's parents that his leg would need to be amputated – he still remembers the 'horror' he felt – and Dorothy signed the amputation order only for a last-ditch effort from an American specialist to save the loss of his leg. This was the first time he was told he could never be a footballer, but it wouldn't be the last.

The Johnston family lived on Lake Macquarie near Fishing Point and his parents doted on their son. He spent his childhood taking tinnies across the water and bush bashing through the Swansea Heads to surf all day. His first love was the sea, and in hindsight he refers to his childhood as being perfect. His father, Colin 'Bruno' Johnston, had tried to earn a contract with Aberdeen in Scotland but failed, because at the age of 24 he was considered to be too old. After years of driving his son around every football pitch in the Hunter Valley, lacing and polishing his son's

Craig Johnston · 127

boots before every game, when the teenager told him he wanted to be a professional footballer Colin was insistent that he do so immediately as he didn't want his son to make the same mistakes he had. Johnston says his father instilled in him 'grit and determination', the two attributes that defined the Australian's career. 'Dad taught me life is all about knowing who you are, where you come from, where you're going and how you'll get there, then shutting up and getting on with it,' Craig told the *Newcastle Herald* after his father's death. 'They don't make them like Dad any more.'

Fifteen years old and thousands of kilometres from professional football, Johnston did the only thing he could: he wrote letters to the major English clubs that told the story of a young boy down under who dominated on the football field and merely wanted a trial. He had luckily seen Middlesbrough play on an Australian tour while at school, otherwise he may never have contacted the only club that replied. It's an unimaginable process today and in 1975 it almost was as well, but in a sense it was fortuitous timing. The Socceroos had appeared at their first World Cup a year prior and had performed with some admiration.

> **Johnston boarded the plane as a sun-swept Aussie surfer, and disembarked as a frightened child in a harrowing London winter.**

A Middlesbrough trainer called Harold Shepherdson took the time to write and post a reply. Boro was a yo-yo club with big ambitions that had just recruited the legendary English footballer Jack Charlton as their manager to instant effect. Times were changing for Boro, so why not crack open the door for an equally ambitious Aussie?

If Johnston paid for his plane fare and accommodation Middlesbrough would give him a trial. This was no easy feat, considering plane fares from Sydney to London in the mid-1970s varied wildly and could cost up to $8000 in today's money. His parents had to sell their house in order to afford the one-way ticket. Johnston boarded the plane as a sun-swept Aussie surfer, and disembarked as a frightened child in a harrowing London winter. Instantly, everything went wrong: he was late travelling to Middlesbrough and didn't have time to find his accommodation or the other triallists; and he travelled straight

Craig Johnston playing for Newcastle KB in the National Soccer League after returning to Australia in 1982.

from the train station to the trial of his life, jet lagged after a 20,000 kilometre plane ride.

'The day before I was on Nobby's Beach, which is a beautiful sandy beach with aqua blue water and palm trees,' he told the BBC. 'Forty-eight hours later I'm on Hutton Road. It was December, it was snowing and it was muddy.' He trialled with the other 15 year olds and Charlton unusually chose to watch the match. His team was down 3-0 at half-time and the famously abrasive manager entered the room and tore shreds off every player. Johnston remembers him being red with rage: 'Managers weren't even supposed to be at trial matches,' he said. Then Charlton turned to Johnston.

'He asked me where I'm from and I said "I'm from Newcastle, northern New South Wales, Australia,"' Johnston said. 'Charlton replied, "Well, you are the worst footballer I have ever seen in my life. You won't make a player while your arse still points to the ground."' Johnston immediately broke into tears and couldn't even play the second half. Suddenly he was not only clubless but homeless, and

> She made him beans on toast and a cup of tea and allowed him to hide out in an old coal shed at the rear of the hotel with a radiator to beat back the biting winter.

was banned from Middlesbrough's trialist accommodation at the Medhurst Hotel. He spent nearly an hour trying to secure a phone

Johnston contests the ball with St George Budapest's Mike O'Shea at Barton Park in 1982.

Johnston and Ian Rush hold the European Cup after beating Roma in 1984.

connection back to his parents, but when they eventually answered he didn't have the heart to tell them that he'd failed so dramatically. When Dorothy asked him how he'd gone he blurted 'He thinks I'm the best footballer he's ever seen' and slammed down the phone. Faced with a broke and sobbing Australian child in the middle of winter, a kind woman who ran the Medhurst took pity on him. She made him beans on toast and a cup of tea and allowed him to hide out in an old coal shed at the rear of the hotel with a radiator to beat back the biting winter. Johnston slept there for the next month, in the process discovering what grit and determination really felt like.

The veracity of Charlton's comments made waves around Boro and the senior players took pity on the young boy they had nicknamed Skippy. Johnston cleaned their boots and washed their cars to make enough money to buy food and spent day after day practising in the Middlesbrough stadium's car park. He had nothing else to do but practise for eight hours per day in the car park, on the street or in the park behind the stadium with the neighbourhood kids.

He was a straggly, unkempt kid but he was wearing professional boots and kicking an authentic first division ball, which the seniors had nicked for him from the dressing rooms. He was taken in by the kindness of Boro's players, especially a particularly kind and talented lad named Graeme Souness.

Although dribbling on tarmac and booting a ball against concrete never made Johnston an excellent player, it did make him unusually tough for his age. When Charlton left Boro in 1977 John Neal took over and was much more receptive to the 'Kangaroo' everyone at the club had fallen in love with. He gave Johnston

Johnston, far right, celebrates with the likes of Kenny Dalglish and Alan Hansen after winning the league title and FA Cup double in 1986.

> ... he said on live British television that 'playing soccer for Australia is like surfing for England'.

his first professional contract and soon realised that while the Aussie wasn't much of a dribbler he had truly fearsome pace. His lungs were like air vacuums, which made him a revolutionary defensive winger who could sprint 100 metres up the pitch to drag away defenders from a crucial attacking move before sprinting the entire length back to charge down a counter-attack. Thousands of shots against a wall in expensive football boots had also developed significant power and accuracy, adding a sense of wonder to an otherwise intensely physical game.

While in one sense Johnston was a brute among the finesse, in another way he brought modernity to the Middle Ages. Everyone else in English football was eating fry-ups and drinking three pints of larger before a game, while Johnston sipped water and ate brown rice. The players used to laugh at him before he outshone them all in a televised match, earning rave reviews above players twice his pay grade and experience. Suddenly, everyone began to take notice. By the end of 1980 the worst player Charlton had ever seen was leading Middlesbrough's scoring with 10 goals in 22 games and was turning back offers from Australia and South Africa to play for England's U/21s.

It was at this stage he said on live British television that 'playing soccer for Australia is like surfing for England'. He has since tried almost everything to retract that statement: he's bashfully apologised, justified it within the context of his love for surfing, blamed Australia's football administration for 'casting him aside' as a youth and explained how leaving England for Australia matches would have destroyed his precarious career. All of these excuses have substance, but the real truth is Johnston never needed Australian football. His immortality is unique because he became the first – and in many ways only – Australian to make European football need him. After 60 appearances and 16 goals at Boro, in 1981 no less than 12 English clubs tried to sign the Australian before Liverpool made him the most expensive signing in the club's history. He rejected a move to Brian Clough's Nottingham Forest and earned Middlesbrough's record transfer fee – £650,000 pounds – to make the most aptly timed transfer in Australian football history. Charlton later said that he 'always knew' the Australian would make it: a backhanded hindsight.

Weeks after his arrival at Liverpool, 20-year-old Johnston sat in the Parc de France stands and watched his new club win the European Cup against Real Madrid, soaking in the enormity of what his future held. His Liverpool side boasted Kenny Dalglish, Ian Rush, Steve Nicol and the player Johnston owed most to: Graeme Souness. Liverpool's quality was a huge step up and Johnston was ignored for much of his first season in, but when he was given a chance 95 minutes into a freezing December night at Anfield against Arsenal, he broke past the Gunners' defensive line and scored, sending Liverpool into the semi-finals of the League Cup, which they eventually won. Towards the end of the 1981/82 season he began to excel in the club's huge occasions, scoring the winner against Manchester United at Old Trafford in front of 50,000 fans and a brace against Forest two weeks later in a brilliant solo performance. His 'lunatic' style quickly made him a fan favourite; nobody in

> His 'lunatic' style quickly made him a fan favourite; nobody in England had seen someone of his ilk before, and the flowing curls and Aussie novelty helped cement his popularity.

England had seen someone of his ilk before, and the flowing curls and Aussie novelty helped cement his popularity. His dismissal of the Socceroos couldn't hamper his impact back home, and he became the first footballer to break into Australian lounge rooms as a regular fixture on Nine's *Wide World of Sports*.

Johnston became the first Australian to win an English league title by the beginning of April 1982, but Liverpool's manager Bob Paisley and the rest of Johnston's team had been so dominant they'd lost their desire. The Reds lost five of their last six games and Paisley left the club. The only player who shone through this period was Johnston: he never gave up and he scored Liverpool's only goals in Paisley's last five matches. In the 1982/83 season his fearsome shot burst into action, and he scored 10 goals in 42 appearances to win his second successive league title and first League Cup trophy, where he was particularly effective in grinding opponents down late into matches. But while Johnston had determination, he never developed self-belief. He later told *The Guardian*: 'You have no idea how crap I was. I was the worst player in the world's best team.'

Liverpool signed prolific midfielder John Wark in 1984 and the Scot went on to outscore Rush, relegating Johnston to just 11 appearances that season while Liverpool won their third title. 'Craig was his own worst enemy,' Dalglish told the *Liverpool Echo*. 'He just didn't believe in his footballing abilities. When his

Johnston fights off three Manchester United players in his typical bulldozer style in 1987.

form deserted him, Craig became depressed and the dark cycle continued. Several times during the season I had to beat away this black dog of depression chasing Craig.'

However, every time Johnston won a chance he made his impact with momentous effect. He played full matches in both of the 1984 League Cup finals as Liverpool beat Everton in a replay. Wark had signed after the UEFA deadline, so Johnston also started the 1984 European Cup final against Roma in front of an incredibly hostile home crowd at the Stadio Olimpico. Roma had bribed the referees throughout the tournament to make it to the final and the club's president was banned for offering the referee €50,000 before the match. The Italian ultras were just as daunting, but 15 minutes in Johnston plunged the stadium into silence. After a tidy one-two combination on the right side he burst down the flank and booted a cross high into the air, foxing Roma's goalkeeper and allowing Liverpool defender Phil Neal to score through the scrummage. It was the most pivotal moment of the 1-1 draw, and while an exhausted Johnston was substituted in the 72nd minute, Liverpool won in penalties thanks to Bruce Grobbelaar's famous wobbly legs.

> Roma had bribed the referees throughout the tournament to make it to the final and the club's president was banned for offering the referee €50,000 before the match.

Johnston playing for Liverpool in his final campaign at the club, in 1987/88. That season he won his second league and FA Cup double.

The Australian had shown yet again that whenever called upon he would deliver, and he cemented himself as a Liverpool immortal the next season. Wark remained at the club but Johnston was irreplaceable, making 41 league appearances and scoring seven goals as Liverpool finished runners-up in four competitions, including the league, in 1984/85. Between 1985 and 1986 there was barely a Liverpool team sheet without Johnston on the wing. He made a whopping 60 appearances as the greatest club on earth won the league and FA Cup double in 1985/86, scoring his most defining goal in the latter. He also scored in the short-lived Super Cup final and scored in the semi-final of the League Cup, but Liverpool couldn't secure a one-off domestic quadruple. Since his arrival he'd played vital roles in Liverpool winning four league titles, two League Cups, an FA Cup and the European Cup. Across multiple coaches, Johnston was one of Liverpool's most consistent big-game players.

The Australian's greatest season was overshadowed by a horrific incident in May 1985. The Reds were playing in Johnston's second European Cup final against Juventus in Brussels' decaying Heysel Stadium. Before kick-off, Liverpool's fans – who were renowned for their passion and, occasionally, violence – stormed through a stadium barrier and pinned Juventus's fans against a retaining wall that collapsed on top of them. The disaster killed 37 people and injured hundreds more. Remarkably, the match still took place in a tense and highly emotional atmosphere as the city entered a state of siege. Johnston played the entire second half but Juventus won, and English clubs were banned from European football for the next five years.

Johnston made 28 appearances and played in another League Cup final in 1986/87, but Liverpool were rendered trophyless for only the second time in his career. In 1987 he worked tirelessly to fight off new competition from prodigious signings such as John Barnes, and he made 35 appearances as he won his fifth league title and made his second FA Cup final. But, ultimately, his career ended as brutally as it began: aged just 27 and still within his physical peak, Johnston's younger sister Faye nearly died while holidaying in Morocco due to a gas leak at her hotel. She was left brain damaged and Johnston immediately retired without warning and returned to Australia. Faye required constant care for the rest of her life and Johnston remained by her side. The 1988 FA Cup final ultimately became his final football match, fittingly against Wimbledon's 'Crazy Gang': one of the only collective of players in football history wilder than himself.

While it was a tragic end to a phenomenal career, Johnston's legacy post retirement has been equally surprising and sensational. After writing 'Anfield Rap', which reached number three in the British charts, he co-wrote 'World in Motion' with New Order. He developed a hotel minibar security system, created an Australian television game show, became a highly regarded photographer, started his own football school and developed the Predator football boot, which sold so well it's credited with saving Adidas from bankruptcy. After all the trials and tribulations, . . . Johnston's record speaks the loudest: he finished his Liverpool career with 10 trophies, 271 appearances and 40 goals and was voted 59th in the club's all-time greatest players. He was the round ball game's first local product to enter Australia's collective sporting consciousness and was the first Aussie footballer to appear on the evening news.

> Johnston's record speaks the loudest: he finished his Liverpool career with 10 trophies, 271 appearances and 40 goals and was voted 59th in the club's all-time greatest players.

Johnston displays the revolutionary football boot he developed, the Adidas Predator.

Club career			
Years	Team	Appearances	Goals
1977–1981	Middlesbrough	64	16
1981–1988	Liverpool	271	40
Honours			
First Division			1982, 1983, 1984, 1986, 1988
League Cup			1983, 1984
European Cup			1984
FA Cup			1986
Charity Shield			1986
Football Federation Australia Hall of Fame			2005
Alex Tobin Medal			2009

Twenty-five-year-old Mark Viduka playing for Celtic in 2000.

MARK VIDUKA

Birthdate	9 October 1975
Place of birth	Melbourne, Victoria
Major teams	Australia, Melbourne Knights, Dynamo Zagreb, Celtic, Middlesbrough
Position	Striker

It's impossible to define Mark Viduka.

In West Yorkshire's medieval suburb of Beeston the Old Peacock Ground was absolutely rocking. The White Rose of York was back in Europe's elite and the sun was shining brightly on Leeds United fans, but up in the executive box their chairman was sweating bullets. Unknown to those below, the club was mortgaged to the hilt to compete with England's giants, and every league loss was pushing them off the White Cliffs of Dover. It was 4 November 2000, Leeds had only won four of their opening 10 matches and they were losing 2-0 at home to Liverpool. Most worrying, they'd splashed £7 million on a troublesome Australian striker who said he was 'too lazy' to play in England and had a record of refusing to play second halves if his club was losing. At that moment, Mark Viduka was just standing there.

Bears may be lazy, but you famously don't poke them. In a moment of madness a Liverpool defender aimed a ridiculous back pass directly at Viduka's feet. While three crazed opponents rushed towards him the Aussie remained painfully still, simply waiting for the ball to reach him before executing the most sumptuous poacher's lob. He turned to the crowd and roared: Liverpool just poked the bear.

Leeds next began to tear down the flank and Viduka, without breaking a sweat, jogged towards the near post and thumped an inch-perfect header into the crack between bar and glove. Liverpool retook the lead but, alarmed by the Australian's casual destruction, thoroughly parked the bus. They lasted 10 minutes before Viduka ghosted behind five opponents to break through on goal. Two players tackled him simultaneously, only for the 188 centimetre, 90 kilogram striker to employ a Maradona turn at full pace (his version includes decking a fullback) before drilling the ball between two centre halves, the goalkeeper and the far post. Elland Road was already in delirium when, 120 seconds later, Viduka killed a teammate's shot with his left boot, slipped it through Liverpool's shell-shocked backline and deftly chipped the goalkeeper with his right. The match ended with Viduka four, Liverpool three.

> He is a true enigma: his talent, achievements and importance are unquestionable yet his personality and motivations are one of Australian football's most alluring mysteries.

Viduka could have been one of the greatest strikers of all time. His four-goal haul to single-handedly beat a treble-winning Liverpool side is the greatest club performance by an Australian footballer. He'd turned just 25 years of age that day and had already scored 119 goals in 180 league games, and he turned down Real Madrid, Barcelona, Manchester United, Inter Milan and Juventus throughout his career. He is a true enigma: his talent, achievements and importance are unquestionable yet his personality and motivations are one of Australian football's most alluring mysteries. He's come to epitomise the most successful and

Mark Viduka's portrait before captaining Australia to the 2006 World Cup.

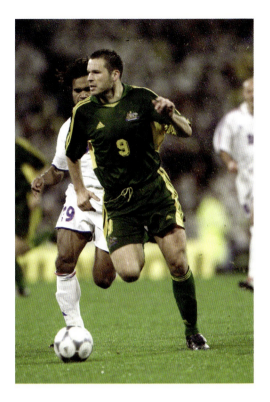

Viduka playing for the Socceroos against France in 2001.

nostalgic aspects of the National Soccer League (NSL), and he was a major Australian pioneer in Europe. While many consider him a divisive, reclusive and unfulfilled figure, it's fitting that his most enduring legacy is captaining the Socceroos at the 2006 World Cup because he was one of the most pivotal footballers Australia ever produced.

Viduka was born to Croatian parents in St Albans in Melbourne's west and was surrounded by a large, well-established Croatian migrant community. His parents had fled war-torn Yugoslavia, where his uncle and grand-uncle had been killed, and passed their longing for an independent Croatia on to their son. Their community had formed Melbourne Croatia (which became the Melbourne Knights) 20 years before Viduka's birth and the club evolved throughout his upbringing to become an NSL giant. Viduka described the Knights to ESPN as a 'symbol of the struggle of free Croatia – free from communism, free from Yugoslavia – and that, for me, meant everything'.

His father took him to watch the Knights when he was three years of age, and he began playing for the club when he was aged six. Their lives revolved around the club – his 'only goal in life was to play for them' – and the club equally relied on its youth. Viduka told FTBL 'nobody really expected too much of me' when he began, but an NSL pathway existed nonetheless. He was naturally tall and strong and was fortunate that former Dinamo Zagreb coach Mirko Bazić was the Knights coach at the time. But it took a Croatian village to raise Viduka: youth dedicate themselves to football across the world, but very few are born into an all-encompassing football club that's dedicated to developing them into a world-class player.

At nine years of age Viduka scored 13 goals in a single game and he began training with the seniors in 1992 when he was aged 16. Between his NSL debut in 1993 and his departure in 1995 he scored an unprecedented 47 goals in 53 appearances. He won the Johnny Warren Medal, U/21 Player of the Year and the NSL's golden boot for both consecutive seasons. In his final campaign he won the NSL Premiership, Championship and Cup treble. He made his Socceroos debut in 1994 at 19 and scored 17 goals in 18 Olyroos caps, including scoring at the 1996 Atlanta Olympics. His talent was as unique as the circumstances that created it; Australia had never seen anything like Viduka and they almost certainly never will again.

'Nearly every game he scored,' Knights teammate Vlado Vanis told *The Age*. 'We knew if we were struggling in defence, we could just hit a long ball and Viduka was there to hold the ball and wait for middle players to come in.' Socceroos defender Steve O'Connor told *The World Game*: 'He also had a fantastic attitude. He was always a terrific player with his feet who could score two or three goals a game regularly. He was so skilful for such a big lad as well. I didn't realise how big he was until I had to mark him.'

Viduka playing against Uruguay in that landmark World Cup qualifier in 2005.

By the age of 20 and amid intense transfer speculation, Viduka was already signalling a different intent: 'I'm not too fond of English football,' he said in 1995. 'I'm sort of a lazy player. I don't really like running that much.' Real Madrid and Juventus knocked, but for the past three seasons and after every goal Viduka had clutched the Croatian crest in his hands and kissed it for the fans. Croatia had declared independence in 1991 and the country's president – who was also president of its leading club, Dynamo Zagreb – personally visited Viduka in Melbourne, so he turned down Europe's giants to join them. Today, Knights Stadium, in the

> 'You will be a symbol to all Croatians,' the president told him, 'one of our own people returning to rebuild our country.'

blighted suburb of Sunshine, consists of three sides of dirt and wooden planks and one pristine grandstand, the Mark Viduka stand, which was paid for by his transfer. He arrived in Zagreb and was heralded by Croatia's president as a national saviour. 'You will be a symbol to all Croatians,' the president told him, 'one of our own people returning to rebuild our country.'

Viduka was expecting the golden stories of his childhood and instead discovered a 'downtrodden' country ravaged by war. '[Fifty] years of communism had left its mark,' he told *The Sunday Times*. He was treated like an outsider, which made him feel more Australian than he ever had before, and he played 10 times for the Socceroos

Viduka celebrates during the penalty shoot-out to decide qualification for the 2006 World Cup.

in 1997 alone, playing in both legs of the infamous 1998 World Cup qualification failure against Iran. He played his first major tournament immediately after, scoring the Socceroos' opening goal of the 1997 Confederations Cup in a 3-1 win against Mexico. He then played every match as Australia made its first major final, but destroyed Australia's chances when he was red-carded after 24 minutes. Brazilian legend Cafu had been tugging his shirt off the ball, and when he skipped past Viduka early the 22 year old hacked his knee directly in front of the referee. Brazil won 6-0.

Viduka was an incredible success in Zagreb, scoring 55 goals in 99 appearances and winning Croatia's best foreigner award and three successive league and cup doubles at the club, but Dinamo's extreme fans turned on their president and hammered his supposed Croatian saviour. Viduka was relentlessly abused in every match and said: 'In the end it turned nasty.' He was never the most determined player, but his love for football was inextricably intertwined with his Croatian identity and the experience devastated him. He may have looked and played tough, but at his heart Viduka was shy and softly spoken. Knights players called him

> 'He came in, took his boots off and went fuck this . . . We couldn't believe it. I thought it was a disgrace.'

'kid' and reminisced about him breaking down in tears while travelling to away games.

Jaded and distraught, Viduka joined Scottish giants Celtic but told the club he needed two month's rest in Melbourne. The notorious Scottish press invented stories that he had quit the club and was in a mental asylum. Despite the baptism of fire, he returned to score an incredible 25 goals in 28 league matches and win Scottish Player of the Year in his only full season at the club. He described Celtic in 2000 as a 'shambles', and in February the club were losing at half-time to second-tier side Inverness Caledonian when Viduka notoriously refused to continue. 'He came in, took his boots off and went fuck this,' Ian Wright told Ball Street. 'We couldn't believe it. I thought it was a disgrace.' Viduka's first transfer 'turned me off football' and his second shattered his reputation, although that match is still best remembered for *The Sun*'s headline 'Super Caley Go Ballistic

Viduka celebrates after scoring a brace for Middlesbrough against Hull City in 2007.

Celtic Are Atrocious'. He may have remained longer at the Hoops but the club reneged on an improved contract. 'If people treat me well, I will treat them better,' he told *The Times*. 'If they double-cross me, they're finished.'

Viduka joined Premier League high flyers Leeds United as one of the club's record signings in 2000, and after explaining to *The Guardian* his English reluctance – 'I'm a big bloke and I really need to get fit' – he exploded into form. He scored four goals against Liverpool in his 11th Premier League match – meaning he made nine goals in five matches – and the game was broadcast live on Australian television. After bashfully admitting he'd done so regularly at the Knights, he turned to the camera, thanked everyone in Melbourne's west and said: 'It means everything to me.'

While 2006 was Australian football's greatest year, Harry Kewell and Mark Viduka's success at the turn of the century changed Australia the most. Kewell's technical finesse had embarrassed England's best in 1999, and now the V Bomber was physically destroying them the following year. He scored 22 goals in 2000/01 and England's perception of Australian footballers changed forever. His performances in the Champions League were groundbreaking, scoring four goals in a single campaign – more than any other Australian has scored in their entire career – to propel Leeds to the semi-finals. He'd always been exceptionally prolific but now there was so much more to his game. He back heeled assists against Lazio, twirled through defenders against Real Madrid, overpowered defenders and earned fouls left right and centre.

After his first two seasons at Leeds he rejected Barcelona, Manchester United and Inter Milan to sign a five-year contract extension. 'I could have gone to Barcelona or Inter Milan but those clubs are slightly unstable at the moment,' he said to *The Times*. 'Why would I want to go to a shitty situation again? Been there, done that. Don't need it.' Leeds teammate Mark Bridges laughed to Optus Sport: 'He was just a lazy, lazy man. He turns up late to training, hops

'He was just a lazy, lazy man. He turns up late to training, hops the fence with jeans and a shirt on, does two laps with the boys, [says] "See ya later, boys, I'm off" . . .

the fence with jeans and a shirt on, does two laps with the boys, [says] "See ya later, boys, I'm off" and the manager let's him do it. He's the big

Viduka, usually very private and reserved, laughs during an Asian Cup press conference in 2007.

Viduka lunges into a tackle against Iraq at the 2007 Asian Cup.

man; he can do whatever he wants. He took my position.'

Ultimately, though, Leeds could never repay his faith. Despite Viduka's incredible goal scoring, the club narrowly missed Champions League qualification twice and went bankrupt without the additional revenue. The entire team was gradually sold off as Viduka twice saved a threadbare side from relegation. In his final season in 2004 his father suffered a brain haemorrhage and he left England midway through a match to return to Australia. Leeds was then finally relegated, and Viduka was bargained to Middlesbrough at 29 years of age and after 72 goals in 166 appearances. He expected Middlesbrough to become a top-six side under his strike power, but he'd given his best years to Leeds and age and indolence had dulled interest from the world's best. When he signed for the Teesiders *The Guardian* cruelly chimed: 'Lazy so-and-so Mark Viduka has found the energy to sign for Middlesbrough.'

As they became European superstars Viduka and Kewell both played rarely for the Socceroos throughout their Leeds tenure and even had a public falling out that Viduka blamed on Bernie Mandic. Viduka made just 12 national appearances in seven years between 1997 and 2005, but the two Australian icons reunited under Guus Hiddink for the Socceroos' famous World Cup qualification campaign. He was both individually devastating and typically unselfish for Australia under Hiddink, scoring an incredible bicycle kick against the Solomon Islands then setting up Australia's goal against Uruguay in the final play-off. Hiddink named him Australia's World Cup captain when Craig Moore succumbed to injuries. He played solidly in every match at the World Cup but was never a regular goal scorer for Australia, and he considered retiring after the tournament at the age of 30. Ultimately he played his best international football in Australia's poorest campaign, the 2007 Asian Cup, scoring three goals only for Australia to fall to Japan in a penalty shoot-out. He scored five goals in six games that year after scoring six times in 37 games over the previous 12. However, after the Asian Cup quarter-final he rejected every national team call up and never played for Australia again.

He returned to his devastating best in his final season, scoring 19 times, but rejected a Middlesbrough extension to join Newcastle United in 2007. His simple explanation was: 'I want to win things.'

With Mark Schwarzer at the back and Viduka up the front, Middlesbrough enjoyed the best period in the club's career. However, not even Big Dukes was immune from Leeds' injury curse. He played against Birmingham on Boxing Day in 2004 and suffered simultaneous back and hamstring injuries that sidelined him for eight months. He returned against the same club in the next season's corresponding match and scored one of the best Premier League goals of all time, beating three players with a double sombrero before volleying from the left edge of the penalty area. He returned to his devastating best in his final season, scoring 19 times, but rejected a Middlesbrough extension to join Newcastle United in 2007. His simple explanation was: 'I want to win things.' He'd helped guide

Viduka celebrates scoring a brace against Thailand in the 2007 Asian Cup.

the club to the UEFA Cup final the previous year and said it had taken him four months to get over losing to Valencia.

While his experiences in Zagreb were heartbreaking, Viduka had found success exceptionally easy at the beginning of his career. He'd won 13 trophies and 11 personal honours by the time he was 25 years old without working nearly as hard as many of his colleagues, but after Leeds' dramatic fall from grace and Middlesbrough's near misses he was suddenly considering his legacy. By the time he joined Newcastle he was 32 years old and had 467 matches in his legs, and it ultimately proved too late. He suffered injuries both midway and then at the end of his first season as Newcastle underperformed. 'I would not be bothered if we lost every game as long as we won the league,' he famously quipped under pressure, but he could see the end was near. 'By his own admission he was going back to Australia at the end of the season and turning it in,' manager Joe Kinnear told Sky Sports. Viduka was a shadow of his former self in his final season, playing 12 matches without scoring. The Australian icon retired without telling anyone, famously stating: 'I didn't tell anyone I was starting, so why tell people when I finish?'

Viduka vanished for the best part of a decade and currently runs a café in Zagreb, telling ESPN his 'only pressure is making a good brew'. Pim Verbeek repeatedly called him up to the Socceroos, which he rejected due to injuries as he tried to reignite his English career; he left football the year before the 2010 World Cup when aged 34. His contradictory nature belies definition but his career spanned an era during which footballers became global brands, and the amount of publicity he generated offers a brief insight into an introverted personality type that's often overlooked. He said his life was 'football, football, football', yet he rarely seemed thrilled about it. His rare interview with the *Herald Sun* in 2011 suggested a footballer not entirely comfortable with his sporting role. 'I have this complex,' he said. 'I don't like too much exposure. I don't know why it is. Maybe it's bred in me, because my dad always told me to be humble and don't think you're too good.'

Like Harry Kewell, Viduka is remembered as being an exceptional talent who never truly delivered for Australia. Perhaps his English fans summarised Viduka's career best, in Alistair Griffin's wistful parody of Leonard Cohen's 'Hallelujah'; it's irreverent but surprisingly beautiful and ever-so-slightly devastating.

I heard there was a secret ball,

Southgate dreamed it would beat them all,

But you don't really play the long ball, do ya?

It goes like this, the full pitch width,

Downing's cross, and Boateng's flick,

The baffled keeper can't stop Mark Viduka.

Mark Viduka, Mark Viduka,
Mark Viduka, Mark Vidu-uu-uka . . .

National career		
Years	Appearances	Goals
1994–2007	43	11
Club career			
---	---	---	---
Years	Team	Appearances	Goals
1992–1995	Melbourne Knights	53	47
1995–1998	Dinamo Zagreb	99	55
1998–2000	Celtic	48	35
2000–2004	Leeds United	166	72
2004–2007	Middlesbrough	103	42
2007–2009	Newcastle United	40	7

Honours	
Johnny Warren Medal	1994, 1995
National Soccer League Golden Boot	1994, 1995
National Soccer League U/21 Player of the Year	1994, 1995
National Soccer League Championship	1995
National Soccer League Cup	1995
Croatian First Football League	1996, 1997, 1998
Croatian Cup	1996, 1997, 1998
Croatian Foreign Player of the Year	1997
Scottish Premier League Golden Boot	2000
Scottish Power Chair Football Association Players' Player of the Year	2000
Oceania Footballer of the Year	2000
Australian Sports Medal	2000
Australian Institute of Sport's Best of the Best	2001
UEFA Cup runner-up	2006
Alex Tobin Medal	2011
Football Federation of Australia Hall of Fame	2014

Sam Kerr runs with the ball for the Matildas against one of their arch-rivals, Brazil, in 2021.

SAM KERR

Birthdate	10 September 1993
Place of birth	East Fremantle, Western Australia
Major teams	Australia, Perth Glory, Sydney FC, Sky Blue FC, Chicago Red Stars, Chelsea
Position	Striker, winger

Many consider Sam Kerr the greatest female footballer in the world; she may yet become the greatest of all time. What's certain is she has changed the face of women's football forever.

What went through Sam Kerr's mind as she led the Matildas out in Grenoble? Was it the 20,000 obligatory chants of Seven Nation Army, the millions of global viewers, the cameras and floodlights and blackened skies shadowing the monstrous Alpine ranges looming overhead? Was it that she, a quintessentially Aussie girl from Fremantle who 'hated soccer' as a kid had just been crowned the best player in the world three times? Was her shell-shocked team, a mess of defensive calamities, yet among the World Cup favourites, weighing on her shoulders? Was she aware that she was not only representing her teammates and her nation but her sport and her gender? Perhaps she knew that her own idols were calling her 'an immature captain' or she was thinking about the 'lesbian mafia' taunt the media were tarring her team with. Maybe she was just considering her response the last time she walked off a football pitch that her critics could 'suck on that one'.

Only Kerr knows. The only thing everyone realised was that it was do or die for the Young Australian of the Year right here against Jamaica. The critics, poppy slashers, creeps, haters and disbelievers were waiting, the whole world was watching, the pressure had reached boiling point and Kerr was about to explode. The Matildas were

One of Sam Kerr's greatest (and most surprising) attributes is her phenomenal heading ability, as she shows against Chile in 2018.

instantly on the back foot against the Reggae Gurlz, one of the World Cup's lowest-ranked teams, but after just 11 minutes Kerr executed a glancing header behind her back to convert a meaningless, looping cross into the game's first goal. She barely celebrated, instead seeming to be driven, almost burdened, that of course it was her and of course it will be her again. Three minutes before half-time she smashed her forehead directly into the ball from point-blank range for her second. She was the most dangerous striker in the world in the most dangerous area of the pitch, and still no one got near her.

Her critics wanted Kerr to be a mature and graceful role model, but she was the best player in the world because when she stepped onto a football pitch she wanted to embarrass her opponents. Her hat-trick couldn't be simpler: she created acres of space, made her marker look useless and side footed the ball harmlessly into the net. However, her fourth goal was the most humiliating, cantering towards the goalkeeper in possession. She feinted out wide to draw the error, stripped the keeper of the ball and slammed it into the net. For the first time in the match she celebrates, like Spartacus: still with clenched fists as the opponent she destroyed lay on

Every other footballer in this book is an Australian football immortal; Sam Kerr is a football immortal.

the ground before her clutching her hands to her face. 'She's a joke. She just shows up, doesn't she, whenever you need a superhero,' Steph Catley said post match.

Australia may never understand what it means to have the greatest women's footballer in the world.

The difference between potential and outcome is the line upon which everything in life is drawn, and on Kerr's line Harry Kewell and Mark Viduka are failures. Every other footballer in this book is an Australian football immortal; Sam Kerr is a football immortal. The difference is in the billions and growing greater every second.

Kerr is one of the best female footballers of all time and Australia's greatest ever footballer of any gender. She's currently 28 years

Sam Kerr, playing for Perth Glory, uses her blistering pace against Sydney FC in the 2019 A-League Women grand final.

of age and merely beginning her career peak yet she's already the most decorated player in Australian history, being the recipient of 30 major individual honours and the winner of 10 trophies. She was named the world's best female footballer in both 2018 and 2019 by the ESPY Awards and in 2019 by *The Guardian*. She's the Matildas' highest-ever goal scorer, exceeding their next best in 51 less appearances. She's a four-time Professional Footballers Association (PFA) Women's Footballer of the Year, Asian Footballer of the Year, the highest goal scorer in National Women's Soccer League (NWSL) history and the most prolific in A-League Women history and the reigning top scorer in the Women's Super League.

'I hated soccer when I was a kid,' Kerr told *The Sunday Times*. 'I never had a soccer ball around the

'I hated soccer when I was a kid . . . I never had a soccer ball around the house.'

Kerr slots home a penalty in the aforementioned grand final.

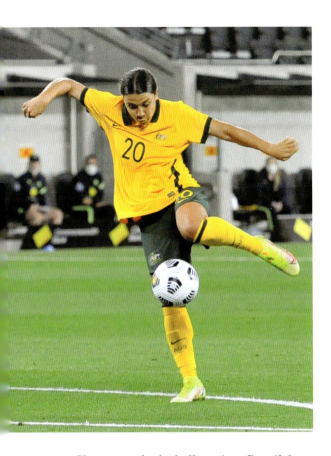

Kerr controls the ball against Brazil for the Matildas in 2021.

house.' She was born to an extremely proud and fiercely competitive sporting family yet also a flawed one. Her grandfather and granduncles on her mother's side were two West Australian Football League footballers and a Melbourne Cup–winning jockey. Her grandfather on her father's side was a featherweight boxer, while her Calcutta-born grandmother was a basketballer. Her father was an AFL footballer, but most notably her brother Daniel Kerr was one of the AFL's greatest players of the 2000s. For many Australians he's still the better-known public figure, but while Sam's career ignited his crashed and burned. He was an athletic sensation derailed by injuries, drug and alcohol struggles and prison sentences. She didn't speak to him for two years, the only way to recall him from the brink. In 2019 he was filmed sculling a beer in a t-shirt reading 'Suck on that'. Daniel is why Sam is the player she is today.

'When my brother played AFL I was young, so being a young kid, growing up with your brother as a professional athlete was awesome,' she told *Just Women's Sports*. 'That's what you want to do. It's your hero playing, then he comes home and it's your brother. So it was just footy, footy, footy for me. After I turned 11 the boys started to grow up a lot, and being a girl I was still tiny, so the first half of the season they were my size, the second half they were huge. I came home with a black eye and a blood lip one day and my father and brother said "Nup, this isn't happening any more." My cousin was playing soccer, they said, "All right, you're going with him." I definitely wasn't excited. In Australia soccer's seen as a sport where people roll around on the ground, it's a sport . . . I don't know what word I can use. You know what I'm trying to say. It wasn't up to me.'

Kerr's devastating attacking arsenal has allowed the Matildas to dominate world-class rivals such as Brazil on multiple occasions.

Kerr brought prodigious athleticism and Aussie Rules physicality to Perth's unexpecting tween girls, and by the age of 13 she had been spotted by legendary Socceroos and Perth Glory striker Bobby Despotovski, who described her talent as 'exceptional'. She made her A-League Women and Matildas debuts within 12 months. She was the fastest, most agile player in every team, so she was let loose on the wing (her brother's AFL position) and played in his wild, unbound style. She scored three goals in three appearances as the Junior Matildas won the ASEAN Football Federation's U/16 Women's Championship, including a brace within 20 minutes of emerging from the bench in the final. In her first A-League Women season in 2009, when aged 15, she was voted the A-League Women's Players' Player of the Year and won Goal of the Year for an awe-inspiring long-range strike against Sydney FC.

'When I first came into under-17s Australia camp . . . everyone was going, "Oh, Sam will be here soon, Sam this, Sam that,"' Alanna Kennedy told Goal. 'I was like, "Who is this Sam that everyone is going on about?" And then she rocked up, the chick from Perth, and she was wild as ever. She's just an unreal athlete, raw talent, and just unbelievably talented.'

> 'When we started this process it was converting two out of eight chances, now she's converting six to seven out of eight.'

Beyond the gift, Despotovski saw the genius: that as a regimented, meticulous striker Kerr could devastate every team in the world. 'We worked very hard on achieving that cool, calm and collected brain to score goals,' Despotovski told Goal. 'Obviously with her speed she's going to separate herself from the defenders quite quickly and then she needs to collect her thoughts and be clear in her mind with what she wants to do with the ball. Year by year, she developed her natural instincts more and more. When we started this process it was converting two out of eight chances, now she's converting six to seven out of eight.'

After making her Matildas debut against Italy – the same nation she'd score her first World Cup goal against exactly 10 years later – Kerr was a constant presence in the squad under Tom Sermanni. She played every match of the 2010 Asian Cup, and in her second competitive Matildas appearance and with her very first touch of the game she scored her debut Matildas goal against South Korea to seal a 3-1 win. It was a shambolic start to a goal-scoring career defined by finesse. The cherubic teenager threw herself in the middle of the penalty box and backed into a clearance that ricocheted into the net before turning and sprinting across the field, spinning a cartwheel and then flinging a backflip before crashing into the mud.

Kerr's second goal a few days later remains the most important goal in Matildas history, and this time it was completely overshadowed. Kerr ghosted behind the North Korean defence – that her coach had previously called 'unbeatable' – defeated their offside trap, sprinted to latch onto a through ball, directed it straight towards goal from the wing and slipped it perfectly past the goalkeeper into the far-side netting. Australia won their first major trophy, male or female, thanks to a 16 year old, and it remains to this day the biggest trophy the Matildas have ever won.

For any other Matilda it would be a career highlight, but for Kerr this was literally just the beginning. She played every match leading into the 2011 World Cup and nearly scored a cracking left-footed volley against Brazil in the tournament's opener. She started both matches and played sensational attacking football as the Matildas beat Equatorial Guinea and Norway back to back to make the quarter-finals, but years of extremely rough AFL, netball and football had destroyed the cartilage in her knees even though she was only 17. When she was sidelined against Sweden, Australia fell apart. She underwent her first knee surgery, which ruled her out for the entire season. While most players would have crumbled, Kerr departed as a pacy raw winger and returned as a world-class striker.

'I think it was sort of during that time [when] she really knuckled down and put in the hard work,' Clare Polkinghorne told Goal. 'Not to say that injuries are a blessing in disguise, but she really made the most of it and she came back a better player, and that's a testament to her and all the hard work that she put in.'

In the 2012/13 A-League Women season Kerr suddenly scored nine goals in just 12 A-League Women matches to win the championship with Sydney FC. Months later she was off to New York to sign for Western New York Flash alongside the greatest striker of all time, Abby Wambach. The NWSL was

> 'Not to say that injuries are a blessing in disguise, but she really made the most of it and she came back a better player, and that's a testament to her and all the hard work that she put in.'

the greatest league in the world until Kerr left it five years later. She mirrored Wambach's versatility and scored six goals as her club won the NWSL Shield and reached the NWSL grand final. She won her first PFA Women's Footballer of the Year award that year at just 20 years of age as well as the Football Media Association's International Player of the Year. The next season she was even greater, usurping Wambach with nine goals in 20 games to finish as the NWSL's second highest goal scorer and assister.

Her then head coach Aaran Lines boasted to *USA Today* that 'with her attributes – her speed, athleticism and instincts – if she continues to develop at the rate she is, Sam can become one of the best strikers in the world'. Kerr said: 'There are times when I think that I'm still a kid and I want to do normal things kids my age do, but I also know this is what I want. I want to be one of those great players no matter what my age is.'

Kerr's desire was tested when she suffered another serious knee injury in 2014 that sidelined her for another seven months and cast serious doubts over her career.

This was a time when the Matildas were lucky to earn $20,000 per year, and she was not only sacrificing her youth but destroying her body for a poor and uncertain future. However, once again, unbelievably, she returned even stronger. She scored an incredible 11 goals in 10 appearances

Kerr has captained the Matildas throughout a landmark era for the team.

for Perth Glory in the 2014/15 season, winning the A-League Women Premiership. She returned to the Matildas to score against France and Italy in 2014 friendlies, and when Alen Stajcic became Matildas coach she transitioned into a main striking role. She played every match as the Matildas once again made the Asian Cup final that year but lost 1-0 to Japan. Kerr ruptured a ligament in her foot before the 2015 World Cup but still returned to play every match, this time as a bonafide world-class star.

Her reputation was becoming so immense in women's football that she was horrifically targeted in the Matildas' second match against Nigeria, when a defender appeared to intentionally try to break her jaw by elbowing her in the face. Again she recovered, playing a key role as Australia won a knockout match at the World Cup for the first time against Brazil, only to once again be denied by a single Japanese goal in the quarter-finals. Following the 2015 World Cup and her third injury return Kerr scored the opener against Germany at the 2016 Olympics, securing a crucial draw that eventually saw Australia progress to another quarter-final. However, she couldn't break the deadlock against Brazil as Australia lost in a penalty shoot-out. This was the end of her injury-scuppered beginning and the beginning of her irrepressible end. Take a breath, because from here on out Kerr becomes completely unplayable.

She scored 10 goals in 13 A-League Women appearances to win the Julie

Kerr has become the Women's Super League's most devastating striker for Chelsea.

> **In 2019 she pioneered a paradigm shift in women's football that would forever change the sport.**

Dolan Medal in 2016/17, then 13 goals in nine appearances in 2017/18 to win it again. Simultaneously, in Australia's winter she traded to New Jersey club Sky Blue, and in her second season set the NWSL record for scoring four goals in a single game to win against Seattle Reign from 3-0 down. In 2017 she scored 17 goals in 22 appearances to become the NWSL's all-time leading goal scorer in just her fifth season, breaking the record for most goals in a single season in the process and winning the NWSL golden boot and the league's most valued player award.

Kerr cemented her place as the world's most prolific striker while also elevating the Matildas to one of the world's greatest teams at the 2017 Tournament of Nations. She entered the tournament with eight goals in 49 Matildas caps and went on to score 11 goals in her next six international games. She scored a hat-trick against World Cup runners-up Japan, then scored once and assisted four times as the Matildas dismantled Brazil to win the tournament to finish as the tournament's highest goal scorer and assister. She won Asian Footballer of the Year that year among a host of other honours too long to mention.

In 2018/19 Kerr began to make the A-League Women look beneath her. She scored a ridiculous 17 goals in 13 games – setting the record for most goals in a season – becoming the A-League Women's all-time leading goal scorer, a record she held for three years after leaving the competition. In the NWSL she traded again to the Chicago Red Stars in 2018 and single-handedly led the side, scoring 16 goals in 20 appearances in her first season and 19 goals in 23 appearances in her second. She was now not only the most prolific striker in women's football but was increasingly regarded as the greatest footballer in the world, voted so three times across those two campaigns. She was also becoming the picturesque face of women's football across the world, signing a ground-breaking deal with Nike that saw her become one of female football's first millionaires.

In 2019 she pioneered a paradigm shift in women's football that would forever change the sport, leaving the NWSL – which

Sam Kerr · 165

had always been the home of elite women's football – to join European powerhouse Chelsea, heralding a new era for the sport. Where Europe's powerhouses had famously derided women's football, the USA had stepped up and professionalised the sport. Now that players such as Kerr were quickly becoming mass-marketed role models, ushered in the same breath as Lionel Messi and Cristiano Ronaldo, Europe was forced to take notice. Women's football would just be football. Like the English Premier League, the English Women's Super League became the greatest league on earth and Kerr its biggest star. In her first full season she scored an incredible 21 goals in 22 league games and 28 goals in 34 total appearances, winning the 2020/21 Women's Super League title, the League Cup, the Community Shield, the WSL's golden boot and made the final of the UEFA Champions League.

In 2019 Kerr spearheaded one of the largest changes in world sport in decades and became one of the most powerful and recognised Australian athletes of all time. However, that year began, as they always do, in January, and in January 2019 the Matildas came crashing down. Under Kerr's exploits they'd been

> Allegations that Stajcic was sacked due a 'toxic' team culture and that a so-called 'lesbian mafia' controlled the dressing room spread like wildfire.

voted Australia's favourite sporting team; they were seen as being both successful and pioneering, angelic and fearsome, but when Stajcic was mysteriously sacked behind closed doors every Matilda was thrust into the spotlight in an entirely new way.

Allegations that Stajcic was sacked due a 'toxic' team culture and that a so-called 'lesbian mafia' controlled the dressing room spread like wildfire, far too alluring not to print. Kerr publicly voiced her support for Stajcic, but suspicion engulfed the entire team. They'd barely been household names long enough to gain fully professional contracts, and suddenly they were experiencing all of its ghastly side effects at once. Just five months later Kerr was named captain of a stunned team heading into the 2019 World Cup. The global media still expected the Matildas to be among the tournament favourites, an unthinkable trajectory in the nation's history let alone after their recent travails. That was how highly

Kerr's backflip celebration, pictured here after scoring against Manchester United in the FA Cup, is one of football's most iconic.

rated Kerr was and she'd never even scored in a World Cup before.

That all changed just 28 minutes into her first match. Her one flaw as a player has always been her penalties and her spot kick against the Italians was saved, but she fortunately scored from the rebound, punching the corner flag in tribute to Tim Cahill. However, her team was a defensive mess and crumbled under the pressure to lose 2-1. The media cycle spun faster and their performance was even worse against arch rivals Brazil, which raced to a 2-0 lead. Then out of nowhere Kerr led the Matildas to the greatest World Cup performance by an Australian side – and one of the best comebacks in Australian sporting history – to score three goals in 15 minutes and win 3-2. Incredibly, Kerr caused both the second and third goals without touching the ball. Brazil was so focused on Australia's talismanic striker that they conceded twice directly from crosses that were aimed at Kerr's head.

'Suck on that one,' Kerr snickered at the media to expectable criticism, but her answer was final. If it wasn't clear enough, her four-goal haul against Jamaica to put Australia through was a more resounding 'bugger off' than anyone expected. She was also demonstrative in the next round against Norway, slicing through the world's fourth-best team in the opening minutes only to narrowly hit the side netting. She earned a penalty for Australia that was ruled out by the video assist referee. Unfortunately, it all came down to Kerr's kryptonite, a penalty shoot-out. She wildly missed her spot kick, skying it into Row Z, and Norway won by the narrowest of margins.

Despite another new coach and a series of horrendous friendly losses, the Australian forward defied the odds to guide Australia to their best performance at the Tokyo 2020 Olympics, finishing fourth. Kerr's first goal against New Zealand set the tone; her second and third goals against Sweden raised the tone (her missed penalty dampening it slightly); her fourth and fifth goals against Great Britain deafened the tone; and her sixth goal against the USA broke all tone-related monitoring equipment whatsoever. She scored enough goals to win a gold medal, but unfortunately the Matildas conceded enough to win a wooden spoon.

Perhaps that will be her lasting legacy, and a signposting of what's to come at the 2023 Women's World Cup. A prodigy before her time, Kerr was born to a nation that can't quite fulfil her potential; maybe it never will. But, disastrous

Kerr applauds the Matildas fans, a vast number of whom she's attracted to the game.

penalties aside, she was one of the leading reasons Australia was awarded hosting rights for the 2023 Women's World Cup, a tournament that may well usurp the Sydney Olympics to become the most-watched event in Australian history. Her exploits forced the world to take Australia seriously on the global football stage just as reluctantly as a blood lip had forced her to take football seriously at the age of 11 – which neatly brings us to her ultimate legacy as an Australian football immortal: drawing tens of thousands of young girls to the world game, whether to reach their full potential or simply toughen it up and stop the rolling around.

National career		
Years	Appearances	Goals
2009–	110	59

Club career			
Years	Team	Appearances	Goals
2008–2011	Perth Glory	22	5
2012–2014	Sydney FC	24	13
2013–2014	Western New York Flash	41	15
2014–2019	Perth Glory	49	52
2015–2017	Sky Blue FC	40	28
2018–2019	Chicago Red Stars	43	35
2019–2022	Chelsea	46	42

Honours	
A-League Women Players' Player of the Year	2009
A-League Women Goal of the Year	2009
Asian Cup	2010
Football Federation Australia U/20 Female Footballer	2010, 2014
A-League Women	2013
Professional Footballers Association Women's Footballer of the Year	2013, 2017, 2018, 2019
Football Marketing Asia International Player of the Year	2013, 2014
National Women's Soccer League Shield	2013
Julie Dolan Medal	2017, 2018
National Women's Soccer League Golden Boot	2017, 2018, 2019
National Women's Soccer League Best XI	2017, 2018, 2019
Asian Footballer of the Year	2017
A-League Women Golden Boot	2018, 2019
Young Australian of the Year	2018
ESPY Best Women's Footballer	2018, 2019
The Guardian Best Footballer in the World	2019
Women's Super League	2020, 2021, 2022
FA League Cup	2020, 2021
Asian Football Confederation Team of the Decade	2020
FA Community Shield	2020
Women's Super League Golden Boot	2021
Women's Super League XI	2021

Lucas Neill, the Socceroos' longest-serving captain, walks out against Costa Rica in 2013.

SUBSTITUTES

LUCAS NEILL

Birthdate	9 March 1978
Place of birth	Manly, New South Wales
Major teams	Australia, Millwall, Blackburn Rovers, West Ham United
Position	Fullback, centre back

National career		
Years	Appearances	Goals
1996–2013	96	1

Lucas Neill deserves to be seen with equal recognition to the greatest Australian footballers of all time. Had he been a striker rather than the most talented defender Australia has ever produced or played for a giant club rather than rejecting the likes of Liverpool, he probably would be. 'His career should be celebrated. He should be a national hero,' Robbie Slater told Sporting News.

Neill's one of the Socceroos' greatest-ever leaders and most diehard servants. He's the Socceroos' third-leading appearance holder with 96 caps, and he captained Australia for the majority of the golden generation era. In this role as a leader of leaders he still appeared a natural, even obvious, choice. He was one of the Socceroos' youngest-ever debutants, played in two World Cups and was man of the match against Uruguay when Australia qualified for its first World Cup in 32 years. He was also one of Australia's greatest Premier League stars and was chased by some of the world's biggest clubs during his peak years. He always excelled as a battling underdog, which elevated him during spells at Millwall, Blackburn Rovers and West Ham United. He was also an incredible rarity among Australians as a Premier League captain.

While other Socceroos won Australian football recognition and respect in the spotlight, Neill won it in the dressing room. His legacy, however, is far more complicated than that of other Socceroos, as his career was full of momentous highs and devastating lows and these contrasts were always the result of his extraordinary aggression. He was a sometimes hated, always feared English Premier League opponent who quickly formed a formidable reputation after breaking English star Jamie Carragher's leg in 2003. His sliding tackle against Italy in 2006 gave away the penalty – rightly or wrongly – that outed Australia from its greatest World Cup campaign. He had a controversial relationship with the A-League, and copped a huge amount of blame for the Socceroos' decline after 2011. This soured his relationship with the fans and media, which erupted in multiple public incidents. He infamously vanished after he was dropped from the 2014 World Cup, disappearing from the public and private eye completely for six years.

Neill's role in establishing the modern Socceroos is momentous, but it remains to be seen what role he can play in Australian football's future.

Neill was best known for his intimidating physical presence and aggressive defensive athleticism.

MELISSA BARBIERI

Birthdate	20 February 1980
Place of birth	Melbourne, Victoria
Major teams	Australia, Richmond SC, Melbourne Victory, Adelaide United, Melbourne City
Position	Goalkeeper

National career		
Years	Appearances	Goals
2002–2015	86	0

'I have 86 caps for Australia, but I'm the last person to leave at the end of training,' Melissa Barbieri said. 'I'm the one to pick up everyone's rubbish off the bench. Do I have to? Of course not, I do it because I respect the club. The parties you miss out on, they're all worth it in the end. People stopped inviting me to parties years ago, partly because I'm not a good dancer, but because they know I won't come.'

Barbieri was part of the Matildas team that made the 2006 Asian Cup final, before she captained the Matildas to win the 2010 Asian Cup in a penalty shoot-out. She has represented the Matildas at four World Cups and the 2004 Athens Olympics, and she's a two-time A-League Women Goalkeeper of the Year who won the second trophy just seven months after giving birth to her first child in 2013. She took over the Matildas' captaincy from Cheryl Salisbury in 2009 and made history by starting for the Matildas at the 2015 World Cup at the age of 35.

'Bubs', as she's known, developed from a 14-year-old girl who 'wasn't able to play as there were no all-girls sides' to a Matildas icon who until the formation of the A-League Women played for Richmond SC as the only female in a semi-professional men's division. She originally began her career as a highly rated midfielder who made state and national squads before a back injury forced her to shift between the posts. In just 12 months she worked her way back into the national team as a goalkeeper.

Barbieri's one of the longest-lived figures in Matildas history, with her loud, outspoken nature and undying desire to play the defining traits behind her success. Only 168 centimetres tall, she still became a ferocious presence between the sticks for the Matildas, just as valuable for her incredible agility as she was for her innate ability to motivate and organise her defensive line. Her remarkably diverse skill set came to the fore when, after suffering a serious hand injury in 2016 following her Matildas retirement, she temporarily transitioned back to playing as a midfielder.

She competed in 18 Women's National Soccer League and A-League Women seasons and is currently an assistant coach at Melbourne City.

Melissa Barbieri is the Matildas' most-capped goalkeeper and an A-League Women's legend.

JOE MARSTON

Birthdate	7 January 1926
Place of birth	Leichhardt, New South Wales
Major teams	Australia, Preston North End, APIA Leichhardt
Position	Centre back, fullback

National career		
Years	Appearances (B)	Goals
1992–2002	13 (37)	0

'Joe showed Australia what our players could achieve,' Socceroo Matt McKay told the Professional Footballers Association. 'He did what many saw as impossible at the time, and Australian players have been chasing that dream ever since.'

Joe Marston was the first Mark Viduka, Lucas Neill, Harry Kewell or Tim Cahill, a pioneer among pioneers: the first Australian footballer to break through overseas and do so in formidable fashion, becoming a Preston North End legend and the first Australian to play in an FA Cup final in 1954. He was named the club's fourth greatest player of all time, making 185 league appearances in just five years before leaving Preston – despite pleas to stay – to return to the country he loved. He played for APIA Leichhardt in the burgeoning New South Wales First Division before retiring in 1969. He managed APIA in three spells and formed a lasting legacy at the club, where the grand stand is named in his honour.

Marston was born in 1926, just six years after the first Australian football team was conceived for a tour of New Zealand. He became the second Australian to play football professionally in England after World War Two, forging the pathway the Australian golden generation would follow 50 years later. Unbelievably, his chance career in England only emerged when Preston's first transfer target refused to leave Australia. Marston was then paid more than double the amount playing for Preston than he received playing for the Australian national team. He became an instant success as a tireless fullback, bringing a complexity and intricacy to a formerly simple role that enabled some of Preston's best years. He spearheaded the club's return to the English first division as a fullback, then gravitated towards the more important role of centre half.

Marston was infamously tough, and stories abound of him training in bare feet in the snow and playing with a broken nose before demanding his opponent straighten it for him. He played 197 consecutive league and cup matches without a day off. He was also extremely highly regarded, being named in the First Division's best XI players during his era. Preston rejected an £80,000 offer from Arsenal for Marston before he returned to Australia at just 28 years of age. He played 37 times for Australia, captaining his country 24 times in an era when international opportunities for Australia were rare and repetitive. He also coached Australia twice as player-coach in 1958 and again in 1966.

Named in his honour, the Joe Marston Medal is awarded to the best player in every A-League grand final.

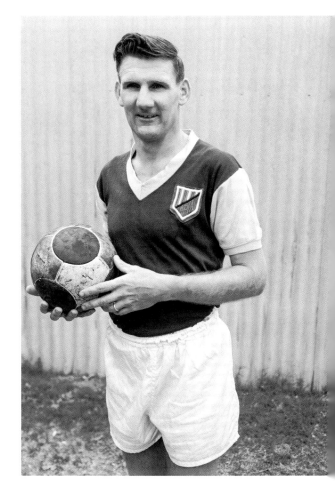

Joe Marston in 1964, in his final year for New South Wales Premiership side APIA Leichhardt.

ALEX TOBIN

Birthdate	3 November 1965
Place of birth	Adelaide, South Australia
Major teams	Australia, Adelaide City
Position	Centre back, fullback

National career		
Years	Appearances (B)	Goals
1988–1998	87 (113)	0

'I believe my Adelaide would have held their own in today's A-League,' Alex Tobin told SBS. 'I am impressed with the way clubs have lifted in terms of professionalism but talented players are talented players whenever and wherever they performed.'

There's good reason the Professional Footballers Association's (PFA's) highest individual honour is named the Alex Tobin Award, presented to players not for their individual brilliance but for the role model they provide and what they give back to the game. Tobin epitomises the ideal that Australian footballers are servants to their country, their clubs, their fans and their sport. In an incredible 522 National Soccer League (NSL) appearances – an Australian football record – he was a pillar of defensive stability, a formidable yet fair and alluring footballer who was typically understated yet capable of marking the world's best. His dedication to the semi-professional NSL, refusing offers to play overseas, remains an inspiration to this day. He was a simple family man who stayed when others left, but he was also an extremely talented professional who set the standards of proficiency and loyalty that represented the best of the NSL.

Tobin began playing for Adelaide City at the age of 19 and made 436 NSL appearances alongside Damian Mori for the club, heralding its proudest decade. He continued to play in the NSL until he was 38, retiring after spells at Parramatta Power and Northern Spirit in 2003. He played 87 A matches for the Socceroos, the most for a generation until Mark Schwarzer, Tim Cahill and Lucas Neill eventually overtook him. None surpassed his 113 total appearances, however, a record that was highly deserved.

He won an Oceania Football Confederation (OFC) Nations Cup with the Socceroos in 1996 as well as three NSL Championships, two NSL Cups and an OFC Champions League title with Adelaide City. His subtle determination and peerless work ethic were the secrets to his longevity and consistency. His passion for the sport is most impressive because his career was defined by the agony of three devastating near misses in World Cup qualification campaigns, yet immediately after their most shattering failure – against Iran in 1997 – his team rebounded to make the 1997 Confederations Cup final. It was a testament to his inspirational leadership.

His retirement in 1998 was a selfless decision that allowed the Socceroos' golden generation – for which he was a guiding light – to take his mantle despite still playing at his peak. He captained Australia for three years, from Paul Wade's retirement until his own. Tobin served as PFA president from 1999 to 2004.

Alex Tobin in 2003, the final year of one of the NSL's most distinguished careers, during his brief spell at Northern Spirit.

HEATHER GARRIOCK

Birthdate	21 December 1982
Place of birth	Sydney, New South Wales
Major teams	Australia, Fortuna Hjørring, Chicago Red Stars, Sydney FC
Position	Midfielder

National career		
Years	Appearances	Goals
1999–2011	130	20

'It makes me really emotional, seeing where we are today and where we've come from, and what the former Matildas had to go through to get to this point,' Heather Garriock told Optus Sport. Thrice a World Cup star, twice an Olympian, an Asian Cup and Oceania Football Confederation Nations Cup champion and the third-most capped Matilda of all time, Heather Garriock is one of the most talented and influential Australian footballers in history.

She made her Matildas debut aged 16 in front of 30,000 fans in China and was an immediate sensation. She played incredibly as a youngster in the Sydney 2000 Olympics, the 2003 World Cup and the 2004 Athens Olympics despite having to work to support herself and enduring the sudden death of her older brother.

She elevates herself to immortal status among extremely stiff competition from fellow Matildas past and present due to her sensational performances in major tournaments. She saved her goals for the most crucial occasions, scoring twice at the 2003 World Cup and again at the 2007 World Cup as well as the winner against Greece at the 2004 Athens Olympics for Australia's first victory at a major tournament. She was instrumental in leading a young Matildas side to win their first and only Asian Cup in 2010.

Garriock won a Women's National Soccer League Championship at 16 then a Julie Dolan Medal three years later. She transitioned from prodigy to pioneer to role model more successfully than almost any other Australian footballer, which made her one of the Matildas' most reliable and admirable stars throughout her career. She was also distinguished as a globetrotter who expanded her international success to club level. She forged a pathway towards professional treatment and helped establish a fantastic reputation for Australian footballers during trophy-laden spells in the USA, Denmark and Sweden. She was equally important to Sydney FC in the W-League, where she won two premierships and a championship.

Garriock's legacy off the pitch has proved almost as important as her achievements on it. She played a vital role in securing the Matildas' first CBA negotiations and later better conditions for Matildas who become mothers after motherhood prematurely ended her career. She was the Matildas' assistant coach under Alen Stajcic, then she coached Canberra United for three years in the W-League. She also started her own football academy and become the first female analyst for men's football matches for an Australian broadcaster.

Heather Garriock fights Ingvild Stensland of Norway for the ball during the FIFA Women's World Cup in Germany in 2011.

DAMIAN MORI

Birthdate	30 September 1970
Place of birth	Melbourne, Victoria
Major teams	Australia, Adelaide City, Perth Glory
Position	Striker

National career		
Years	Appearances	Goals
1992–2002	45	29

'When you are that far out you just hit it. I guess I got lucky, because from that distance no-one really means to put it in.' The referee's shrill whistle, Joe Mullen's nonchalant tap, Mori lifting his arms, swinging his right boot and slicing the second touch of the game into the air. The stunned silence of 4,000 people became gasps and then gulps, then an explosion of cheers as the ball travelled 60 metres across Hindmarsh, dipping just above Josh Perosh's sprawling arms for the world-record fastest goal in football league history.

To this day Damian Mori's 1996 National Soccer League (NSL) goal directly from the kick-off against Sydney United remains the fastest and most incredible goal scored on Australian soil. It took just 3.69 seconds for Mori – Australia's greatest domestic striker, who heralded a new age for the Socceroos – to prove he was the 1990s' most fearsome forward. Over the next few months he set a still-standing record of 33 goals in a single season, won the first of two Johnny Warren medals and secured a move to one of Europe's strongest leagues. He never became a global striker, but he brought global striking to Australia.

Mori scored over 300 goals in nearly 600 professional league appearances, playing for five NSL sides and top scoring in five separate seasons. He's the second-highest Socceroos goal scorer of all time with the best goal to game ratio of any Australian striker in the top 10. He couldn't break through at German powerhouses

Borussia Mönchengladbach, but for Australian football fans in the 1990s and early 2000s he was the greatest striker Australia had ever seen. He won an NSL Cup with South Melbourne in 1989 before Ferenc Puskás gave him the boot, then played every match as part of the Olyroos' greatest Olympic team, finishing fourth in Barcelona in 1992 and heralding a new era for Australian football.

Mori won an NSL Championship with Adelaide City in 1993 then scored an unprecedented 31 goals in 36 games in 1995/96. His crowning glory with the Socceroos was in 1997, when he played an important role as an impact substitute in Australia's dream run to the final of the 1997 Confederations Cup. He described himself as a 'box striker' and had the mentality and positional awareness of a poacher but a dream array of physical attributes that defied any simple label. He won two NSL Championships back to back with Perth Glory between 2002 and 2004, partnering Bobby Despotovski to Australian football's most devastating attacking partnership. Mori likely would have dominated the A-League in similar fashion had coaching and business interests not captured his heart.

Damian Mori during one of his brief but highly successful A-League spells at Central Coast Mariners in 2006.

PETER WILSON

Birthdate	15 September 1947
Place of birth	Gateshead, England
Major teams	Australia, Middlesbrough, Western Suburbs, APIA Leichhardt
Position	Centre back, sweeper

National career		
Years	Appearances	Goals
1970-1979	65	3

'He is the toughest man I've played against. He didn't seem to care whether he kicked a ball, a leg, or a head.' Those were the words of German icon Gerd Müller about the Socceroos' first World Cup captain Peter Wilson. Wilson was one of the toughest and most intimidating defenders of his era, however, many also believe that he was the greatest Socceroo ever at the time. He brought fierce physicality to a highly athletic and tactical role as Australia's libero at the 1974 World Cup, and after that tournament many European newspapers regarded him as being one of the finest defenders in the world. He played 65 official Socceroos matches and an enormous 133 total Australian matches, including test games.

Australia's first World Cup coach Rale Rasic described Wilson as 'a fascinating character with incredible authority and understanding'. He was a mountain of a man with a huge, ripped chest, flowing gold locks and a thick handlebar moustache. He was also extremely shy and, with Lucas Neill, sets a tradition for aggressive Australian defenders to shun football and the spotlight entirely post retirement. Today he's reported to be a heavily tattooed biker recluse who has barbed wire fences surrounding his mountain hideaway and who lost his love for football decades ago.

Wilson was born in Gateshead, England but failed to break into Middlesbrough, so he migrated to Australia as many failed English footballers did at the time. He switched to the sweeper role after the first of many injuries during his career and quickly became an immense force in the New South Wales First Division. He won his only championship with Marconi in 1972 but spent the majority of his career at South Coast United, Western Suburbs and APIA Leichhardt, making 299 professional league appearances from 1966 to 1982.

Wilson played under Johnny Warren's captaincy for his first three years with the Socceroos, playing in Australia's notorious 1970 Vietnam tournament victory. He then took the leading role to sensational effect after Warren's injury and ultimately captained the Socceroos 60 times. He commanded Australia to become champions of Oceania and Asia in 1973, beating Iraq, Indonesia, New Zealand, South Korea and Iran en route in one of Australian football's greatest success stories.

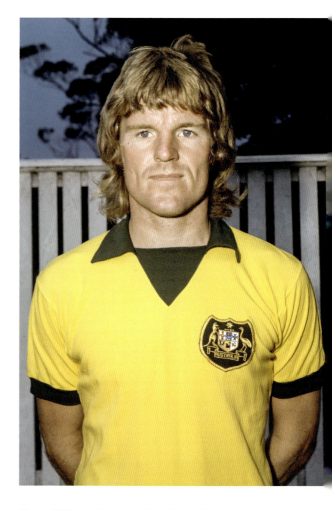

Peter Wilson (pictured without the handlebar moustache) was Australia's most fearsome footballer.

He played arguably the greatest personal World Cup campaign in Socceroos history the following year in Germany, ensuring his part-time Australian side retained respectability against both the East and West German national teams on their home soil before his defensive solidity won Australia its first World Cup point in a 0-0 draw against Chile.

Australian captain Peter Wilson and Israeli captain Zvi Rosen at Olympic Park, Melbourne ahead of the final game of a three-match series in 1971

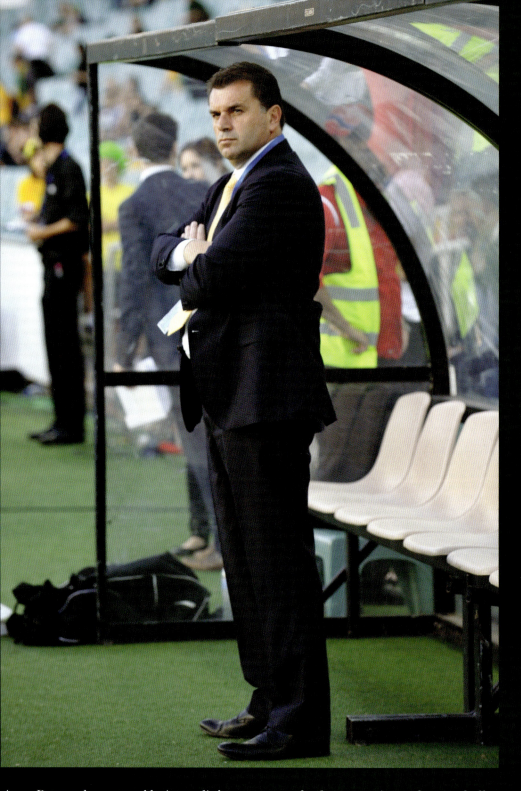
Ange Postecoglou, arguably Australia's greatest coach of any sporting code, marshalls the Socceroos against Costa Rica.

COACH
ANGE POSTECOGLOU

Birthdate	27 August 1965
Place of birth	Athens, Greece
Major teams	Australia, South Melbourne, Brisbane Roar, Yokohama F Marinos, Celtic
Position	Coach, defender

'At Brisbane it was about playing a different way, what people call high-risk play, playing out from the back,' Postecoglou told the ABC. 'It was a foundation for us. We came down here to play Victory and whenever you play Victory it's a big deal, but for me it was even bigger, coming back to my home town, the first time my family had seen us play in a long time, with this new Brisbane team. I felt the pressure and wanted to show people the team we had built.

'We started the game and Luke DeVere, who was this young centre back at the time, got the ball, tried to play out from the back; it got cut out and Victory score. Same thing happens again: Luke DeVere gets the ball, and instead of just booting it out of the park he's trying to play and we cop a second. We end up losing 3-0. I remember at the time it was a real seminal moment because I'm thinking, "He's doing exactly what I want him to do." As gutted as I am [at] losing – and I'm not a good loser, especially in that scenario – I had to come in, and I was so proud of him that I thought, "I've got these guys now. If they're prepared to do that, a young guy after coughing one up and costing us a goal will do exactly the same thing again in front of 25,000 people the next time around, I've got him now."

'I walked in there and said: "Mate, I couldn't praise you higher. That sort of courage will give us success." It was the last time we lost for 36 games.'

Those 36 games from 2011 to 2012 comprise the longest undefeated streak in Australian professional sporting history for any code. Today, however, they're merely the first of the many insurmountable barriers Ange Postecoglou has smashed in a uniquely pioneering career. He's accomplished more for Australian football as an individual than almost any other in the sport's history. A South Melbourne legend and Socceroo who has become the most successful Australian coach of all time, Postecoglou brought the beautiful game to Australia and revolutionised Australia's expectations, insisting to a country in which many don't want to take part that they can rule the world.

Postecoglou emerged from semi-professionalism and arduous, reputation-thrashing failures to bring a dangerous, aggressive philosophy to the National Soccer League (NSL), the A-League and the Socceroos, then the pinnacle of Asia and now to the European elite. As a coach he's won two NSL Championships, two A-League Championships, Australia's first major international trophy at the 2015 Asian Cup and the first major foreign league title by an Australian coach in the 2019 Japanese J-League.

He's since become the first Australian to coach a major European club with Scottish giants Celtic. He was awarded Asian Coach

> 'I brought home the Asian Cup, showed it to him and he said: "If you made a substitution you wouldn't have had to go to extra time."'

of the Year and the Professional Footballers Association's Manager of the Decade in 2015, but after 25 years of coaching and at the age of 56 his career is just getting started. His self-belief is among the most notable in Australian sport; it's why he's won seven out of seven championship finals during his career.

Postecoglou was born in Greece but grew up in the inner-city Melbourne suburb of Prahran, where he fell in love with neighbourhood cricket and showed an aptitude for AFL. His father, a stereotypical hard-working, chain-smoking Mediterranean émigré, wouldn't have a bar of any sport but football. When Postecoglou brought home an AFL trophy one afternoon his father said 'That's it' and dragged him into the backyard to play football.

For Postecoglou the world game was destiny. 'The only way I could be close with [my father] was this sport,' he said. 'There was no other connection between me and him.

Postecoglou, pictured coaching Australia against South Africa, has always had a strained relationship with the media.

I brought home the Asian Cup, showed it to him and he said: "If you made a substitution you wouldn't have had to go to extra time." After the World Cup – where I thought we did all right – I got him a really nicely bound book . . . I said: "It's all the photographs from the World Cup, it's my experience, a personal thing," and he said: "Oh, yeah, that's the team that didn't win any games." He thinks that's the only thing that will motivate me, and it's worked well so far.'

Postecoglou began captain-coaching his high school football team in Year Seven and ultimately coached the team all the way through high school, winning a Victorian state championship. He believes his tactical nous took him further in his playing career than his physical abilities deserved. He wanted to be a commanding midfielder but was relegated to defence at South Melbourne, and he became renowned for his attacking intent from the back line. He's now regarded as being one of the greatest South Melbourne players in the club's history, marshalling the team to two NSL Championships. He played 193 NSL games for the club during its proudest years, forming his coaching passion under the likes of Ferenc Puksás, Frank Arok and Rale Rasic. 'My playing

Postecoglou with the Socceroos team he guided to the 2015 Asian Cup.

career was a real struggle,' he said. 'I just knew I wasn't that good. My playing career was just waiting to start my coaching career.'

Within three years of retiring Postecoglou was coaching South. 'We had a strong British influence, and obviously it was a pretty basic form of the game,' he told ESPN. 'So then when we saw it didn't work we looked at other approaches and said: "Let's go Dutch or let's go German or Brazilian or whatever." But the point we kept missing was that to grow we had to be Australian, because that's who we are. You can learn from others but you have to be yourself. You can't start out with the idea that you have to copy others; you have to play to your strengths.'

Most coaches believe that Australia's strength is in their physicality so they favour defensive, resolute football, whereas Postecoglou believes defending is the antithesis of the Australian underdog mentality. If Australians believe they can take on anyone and anything then an Australian team should be in their opponent's face, pressing high and pushing forward at every opportunity.

Postecoglou's South side was famed for forceful rapidity, but aggression is easier when you're a big fish in a small pond. He won the Oceania Football Confederation Champions League 5-1 against a Fijian club in 1999, sending his bunch of part timers to the Club World Cup to face the likes of Manchester United. They lost every

> 'You just do what you think is right and over time you'll see whether you're successful or not ... There's a core belief within you that you constantly fall back on.'

match but drew praise for their utter fearlessness. It was a hint of what was to come.

Postecoglou's next test came with the Australian U/17 and U/20 sides. He took teenagers who were barely playing at senior level into humid, sodden, foreign Asian territory against bus-parking minnow opposition and was sacked after failing to qualify for two junior World Cups. He later admitted that his biggest regret was succumbing to the pressure to change his style. 'You just do what you think is right and over time you'll see whether you're successful or not,' he said. 'There's a core belief within you that you constantly fall back on.'

He joined Brisbane Roar in 2009 and told the club he wanted to be judged in a year, as he rebuilt an ageing squad – cutting Socceroos and foreign stars alike – and transformed a young team into 'Roarcelona'. Playing football described as the best the A-League had ever seen, he won the 2011 and 2012 A-League Championships during the longest undefeated streak in Australian sport.

He took over the Socceroos at their lowest ebb in 2014. The golden generation had dissolved, suffering successive 6-0 losses against France and Brazil. At the 2014 World Cup Postecoglou's fledgling team was drawn into a group of death against Chile, the Netherlands and Spain. They lost every match, but they lost fearlessly. The next year the same team scored 14 goals in six games to win the 2015 Asian Cup in extra time. It was Postecoglou's seventh win in seven tournament finals.

His attacking ethos with the Socceroos wasn't about destroying teams but about grinding them into submission by dominating the ball, forcing their opponents to continually track overloads and defend for long periods. He guided the Socceroos through the longest qualification campaign in World Cup history between 2016 and 2017: they played 22 erratic matches and travelled 250,000 kilometres – the most matches and the furthest distance a team has ever endured to qualify for a World

Postecoglou walks amid a field strewn with confetti after winning Australia's first and only major football trophy.

Cup – and eventually prevailed, only for Postecoglou to quit the Socceroos before seeing his project to fulfilment.

In four years he rebuilt the team, transformed its style, won their first major trophy and raised them 52 places in the FIFA world rankings. Still, the old Hollywood adage 'You're only as good as your last performance' perfectly suits the theatrics of modern sport. The relentless pressure to win at all costs was a sign Postecoglou's latest project had come to an uneasy conclusion. Within two months he joined Japanese club Yokohama F Marinos and won their first league title in 15 years, scoring 22 more goals than second place. He was then named manager of Scottish giants Celtic, one of the most supported and recognised clubs in world football, and against every odd and a storm of global disbelief, led the European giants to the Scottish Premier League title in his first season. This achievement puts him in glorified air among Australian coaches of any discipline, and further cements his place as a revolutionary figure in the nation's football history.

Australian football's male flag bearer is no longer a physical athlete but a bristling middle-aged tactician. Thanks to him, who knows what will happen next.

Managerial honours	
National Soccer League Premiership	1998
National Soccer League Coach of the Year	1998
National Soccer League Championship	1998, 1999
Oceania Club Championship	1999
Australian Sports Medal	2000
Oceania Football Confederation U/20 Championship	2001, 2002, 2005
Oceania Football Confederation U/17 Championship	2001, 2003, 2005
ASEAN Football Federation U/19 Youth Championship	2006
A-League Premiership	2011
A-League Championship	2011, 2012
Asian Cup	2015
Professional Footballers Association Manager of the Decade	2015
Asian Football Confederation Coach of the Year	2015
J-League	2019
Scottish Premier League	2022

BIBLIOGRAPHY

Mark Schwarzer

John Greco, Arsenal star's compliment to Aussie trailblazers, My Football, 2017, https://www.myfootball.com.au/news/arsenal-stars-compliment-aussie-trailblazers, accessed 7 August 2021.

Hans and Doris Schwarzer, Meet the Families: Mark Schwarzer, Migration Heritage NSW, 2015, https://web.archive.org/web/20150718060750/https://www.migrationheritage.nsw.gov.au/exhibitions/worldcup/family-schwarzer.shtml, accessed 7 August 2021.

Schwarzer's Return to Dresden, Optus Sport Originals, 2020, https://sport.optus.com.au, accessed 7 August 2021.

Alex Zaia, How Karmara orchestrated Schwarzer's maiden Premier League transfer, SEN, 2020, https://www.sen.com.au, accessed 7 August 2021.

Jake Rosengarten, Guus Hiddink finally tells Mark Schwarzer: Croatia axing for Kalac was a mistake, Optus Sport, 2019, https://sport.optus.com.au, accessed 7 August 2021.

Dominic Fifield, 'Mark Schwarzer enters his 40s fit, in form and focused on Fulham', *The Observer*, 2012, https://www.theguardian.com, accessed 7 August 2021.

Jamie Jubert, 2019, Ex-Chelsea and Fulham keeper Mark Schwarzer on his career and life in Surrey, Get Surrey, 2019, https://www.getsurrey.co.uk, accessed 7 August 2021.

Mile Jedinak

Books

Deans, Adrian, *Political Football: Lawrie McKinna's Dangerous Truth*, High Horse Books, 2018.

Websites

The AFC, https://www.the-afc.com/news/afcsection.

Ray Gatt, Family values, work ethic give Socceroos worthy leader in Jedinak, news.com.au, 2014, https://www.news.com.au, accessed 5 August 2021.

David Davutovic, Mile Jedinak's long journey from struggling part-time player to World Cup captain, Adelaide Now, 2014, https://www.adelaidenow.com.au, accessed 5 August 2021.

Dominic Bossi, 'Mile Jedinak just enjoying the moment of the Asian Cup final', *The Sydney Morning Herald*, 2015, https://www.smh.com.au, accessed 5 August 2021.

AAP, 'Former Central Coast Mariners coach Lawrie McKinna told not to sign Mile Jedinak', *The Sydney Morning Herald*, 2015, https://www.smh.com.au, accessed 5 August 2021.

FFA Media, From the NSL to the Premier League – FFA acknowledge Mile Jedinak, My Football, 2020, https://www.myfootball.com.au, accessed 5 August 2021.

Cheryl Salisbury

Scott Bevan, 'Cheryl Salisbury kicks goals in life', *Newcastle Herald*, 2017, https://www.newcastleherald.com.au, accessed 2 July 2021.

Brittany Mitchell, 'We were playing for the love of the game': Matildas great Cheryl Salisbury, ESPN, 2019, https://www.espn.com.au, accessed 2 July 2021.

Hamish Macdonald, The Year That Made Me: Cheryl Salisbury, 2002, ABC, 2017, https://www.abc.net.au, accessed 2 July 2021.

Erin O'Dwyer, 'It's not a fair game, boys', *The Sydney Morning Herald*, 2008, https://www.smh.com.au, accessed 2 July 2021.

Caroline Wilson, 'A naked desire to win some credibility', *The Sydney Morning Herald*, 2000, www.olympics.smh.com.au, accessed 2 July 2021.

Johnny Warren

Books

Fink, Jesse, *15 Days in June: How Australia became a football nation*, Hardie Grant Books, 2007.

Warren, Johnny with Andy Harper and Josh Whittington, *Sheilas, Wogs and Poofters: An Incomplete Biography of Johnny Warren and soccer in Australia*, Random House Australia, 2003.

Websites

Daniel Lane, 'When the Socceroos won behind enemy lines', *The Sydney Morning Herald*, 2014, https://amp.smh.com.au, accessed 29 June 2021.

Sivan John, Wogs, Poofters & St. Johnny Warren: The Patron Saint of Australian Soccer, Football Paradise, 2017, https://www.footballparadise.com/wogs-poofters-story-of-st-johnny-warren-patron-saint-of-australian-soccer, accessed 29 June 2021.

Julie Dolan

Barbara Cox, A brief history of women's football until 1991, WeAreAsia, 2000, www.weareasia.com/en/women/about/, accessed 9 July 2021.

Harry Kewell

Paul Gough, Kewell hits back at critics, Sportal, 2010, https://sportal.com.au, accessed 23 June 2021.

Michael Lynch, 'The man behind Harry Kewell: who is Bernie Mandic?', *The Sydney Morning Herald*, 2016, accessed 23 June 2021, https://www.smh.com.au.

AAP Newswire, Harry Kewell speaks of injury nights, Liverpool and his coaching aspirations, ESPN, 2016, https://www.espn.com.au, accessed 23 June 2021.

Paul Connolly, 'Harry Kewell: from Sydney's west to the grandest stages of world football', *The Guardian*, 2016, https://www.theguardian.com, accessed 23 June 2021.

Staff writer, The Long Read: Harry Kewell, PFA, 2018, https://pfa.net.au, accessed 23 June 2021.

Staff writer, The men who made Harry, FTBL, 2009, https://www.ftbl.com.au, accessed 23 June 2021.

Tim Cahill

Ray Gatt, 'Tim Cahill rated "the greatest Socceroo" by Rale Rasic', *The Australian*, 2008, www.theaustralian.news.com.au, accessed 2 August 2021.

Stephen Farrelly, Interview: Tim Cahill returns to FIFA 22 as a Hero, Red Bull, 2021, https://www.redbull.com, accessed 5 August 2021.

Amy Cooper, 'Tim Cahill bows out of soccer with a thank you to his doubters', *The Sydney Morning Herald*, 2018, https://www.smh.com.au, accessed 2 August 2021.

Charlie Carmichael, 'How a defiant upbringing elevated Tim Cahill to Premier League Stardom', *These Football Times*, 2017, https://thesefootballtimes.co, accessed 5 August 2021.

Lisa De Vanna

Craig Foster, 'How we learned to live dangerously', *The Sydney Morning Herald*, 2007, https://www.smh.com.au, accessed 28 July 2021.

Samantha Lewis, 'Lisa De Vanna: "Every player wants to have that heroic send-off"', *The Guardian*, 2020, https://www.theguardian.com, accessed 28 July 2021.

Tom Smithies, De Vanna pays tribute to father, Fox Sports, 2021, https://www.foxsports.com.au, accessed 28 July 2021.

Tony Harper, Matildas captain Lisa De Vanna on her controversial career and pride in being named to lead her country, Fox Sports, 2021, https://www.foxsports.com.au, accessed 28 July 2021.

Ann Odong, De Vanna: 'We really wanted to make a statement as a nation', Matildas, 2020, https://www.matildas.com.au, accessed 28 July 2021.

Lisa De Vanna, From Dole Queue to A Dream, AthletesVoice, nd, https://www.athletesvoice.com.au, accessed 28 July 2021.

Dominic Bossi, Women's World Cup: How Lisa De Vanna went from problem child to captain of Matildas, *The Sydney Morning Herald*, 2015, https://www.smh.com.au, accessed 28 July 2021.

Lucy Zelic, There's something about Lisa, SBS, 2015, https://www.sbs.com.au, accessed 28 July 2021.

Lisa De Vanna, Matildas' Lisa De Vanna on Matildas & Cheryl Salisbury, PlayersVoice, nd, https://www.playersvoice.com.au, accessed 28 July 2021.

Michael Lynch, '"I don't hide who I am": why Matilda Lisa De Vanna divides opinion', *The Sydney Morning Herald*, 2019, https://www.smh.com.au, accessed 28 July 2021.

Richard Parkin, 'Lisa De Vanna: "I used to lose my mind about simple things"', *The Guardian*, 2019, https://www.theguardian.com, accessed 28 July 2021.

ESPN, The Matildas, 2013, www.espn.com.au/aussies-abroad-2, accessed 28 July 2021.

Craig Johnston

Craig Foster, 'I was cast aside – Skippy sets the record straight', *The Sydney Morning Herald*, 2009, https://www.smh.com.au, accessed 15 July 2021.

Matty Jones and Matty Nixon, Liverpool FC star Craig Johnston: 'Jack Charlton said I was the worst player ever', BBC, 2020, https://www.bbc.com, accessed 15 July 2021.

Stuart Jeffries, 'Magic Johnston', *The Guardian*, 2004, https://www.theguardian.com, accessed 15 July 2021.

FourFourTwo staff, Craig Johnston: Q&A, FourFourTwo, 2008, https://www.fourfourtwo.com, accessed 15 July 2021.

Damon Cronshaw, 'Football great Craig Johnston returns for father's funeral', *Newcastle Herald*, 2012, https://www.newcastleherald.com.au, accessed 15 July 2021.

Damon Cronshaw, 'Liverpool great Craig Johnston celebrates from Newcastle as his team win the league for the first time in 30 years', *Newcastle Herald*, 2020, https://www.newcastleherald.com.au, accessed 15 July 2021.

Damon Cronshaw, 'Liverpool legend Craig Johnston opens up about life and leaving a legacy', *Newcastle Herald*, 2016, https://www.newcastleherald.com.au, accessed 15 July 2021.

Mark Viduka

Joe Gorman, 'Former Socceroo captain Mark Viduka will never forget his roots', *The Sydney Morning Herald*, 2015, https://www.smh.com.au, accessed 13 August 2021.

Staff writer, Kinnear feared for Viduka, Sky Sports, 2008, https://www.skysports.com, accessed 13 August 2021.

Michael Bridges, Michael Bridges has a dig at Lazy Mark Viduka/GegenPod, Optus Sport, 2021, https://www.youtube.com, accessed 13 August 2021.

Lucas Radbourne, The 10 most brilliant Mark Viduka quotes, FTBL, 2020, https://www.ftbl.com.au, accessed 13 August 2021.

Staff writer, 'Viduka pledges to play on for Australia', *The Sydney Morning Herald*, 2005, https://www.smh.com.au, accessed 13 August 2021.

Amy Lawrence, 'Viduka leaves the asylum', *The Guardian*, 2000, https://www.theguardian.com, accessed 13 August 2021.

Joe Gorman, 'Mark Viduka: the Socceroos great whose Croatian roots ran deep', *The Guardian*, 2017, https://www.theguardian.com, accessed 13 August 2021.

Michael Cain, Exclusive: Mark Viduka breaks his silence on Leeds, the Socceroos and Lucas Neill, ESPN, 2020, https://www.espn.com.au, accessed 13 August 2021.

Trevor Treharne, How Dukes Made His Mark, FTBL, 2011, https://www.ftbl.com.au, accessed 13 August 2021.

Greg Baum, 'Viduka: an Australian story', *The Age*, 2000, https://www.melbourneknights.com.au, accessed 13 August 2021.

Sam Kerr

Ameé Ruszkai, The transformation of Australia's Sam Kerr: From wild winger to best No.9 in women's football, Goal, 2019, https://www.goal.com, accessed 2 August 2021.

Staff writer, 'Didn't speak for two years': Sam Kerr lifts lid on falling out with brother, Yahoo Sport, 2019, https://au.sports.yahoo.com, accessed 4 August 2021.

Staff writer, 'An immature captain' – Former Matildas question Kerr's comments, Goal, 2021, https://www.goal.com, accessed 4 August 2021.

Jeff DiVeronica, 'Samantha Kerr shines for WNY Flash', *USA Today*, 2014, https://www.usatoday.com, accessed 4 August 2021.

David Mark, Independent review says no lesbian mafia in Matildas, Alen Stajcic removal not personal, ABC, 2019, https://www.abc.net.au, accessed 4 August 2021.

Melissa Barbieri

Lucas Radbourne, Leading by example: Barbieri urges youth to grasp chance, The Corner Flag, 2015, https://www.cornerflag.com.au, accessed 12 September 2021.

Heather Garriock

Jacob Windon, Heather Garriock Q & A: Iconic moments, powerful stories, and 'never celebrating wins', Matildas, 2019, https://www.matildas.com.au, accessed 12 September 2021.

David Weiner, Optus showing us playing live all the time is massive for young girls in Australia, Optus Sport, 2021, https://sport.optus.com.au, accessed 12 September 2021.

Alex Tobin

Staff writer, One small step for Alex Tobin, one large chapter for the record books, *The Sydney Morning Herald*, 2003, https://www.smh.com.au, accessed 23 July 2021.

Damian Mori

Simon Hill, Simon Hill chats to Damian Mori about his career in the NSL and A-League and his coaching ambitions, Fox Sports, 2021, https://www.foxsports.com.au, accessed 12 September 2021.

Phillip Micallef, Socceroos Greats – Where are they now: Damian Mori, SBS, 2017, https://www.sbs.com.au, accessed 12 September 2021.

Joe Marston

Staff writer, Obituary, Joe Marston: Bradman of soccer blazed the trail for Australian players, *The Sydney Morning Herald*, 2015, https://www.smh.com.au, accessed 26 July 2021.

Peter Wilson

Staff writer, 'Wilson's quiet word on Socceroos', *The Age*, 2006, https://www.theage.com.au, accessed 12 September 2021.

The Southern Cross, Peter Wilson, https://www.peterwilson.info/games.htm, accessed 12 September 2021.

Ange Postecoglou

Santo Cilauro and Sam Pang, Summer Series: Ange Postecoglu, ABC, 2017 https://www.abc.net.au, accessed 8 August 2021.

Gabriele Marcotti, Ange Postecoglou is a formidable character, who is reviving Australia, ESPN, 2016, https://www.espn.com.au, accessed 8 August 2021.

ACKNOWLEDGEMENTS

This book would have been monotonous to research without the many litterateurs who have elevated Australian football journalism over the decades. It would have been painstaking were it not for the statistical beauty of the OzFootball archive and without Kevin Airs, who fulfilled so many of my professional aspirations. Finally, it wouldn't have been possible at all without my family, who deserve all the remaining credit for anything I accomplish.

Viduka celebrates a goal for Newcastle United against West Ham United at St James' Park, Newcastle in 2007.

ABOUT THE AUTHOR

Lucas Radbourne thinks he could have gone pro if it wasn't for his bad knee. Instead, he settled for being an editor for FourFourTwo Australia, FTBL, The Women's Game and *Beat Magazine*. He's also a director of a non-profit foundation and has been published in *The Guardian*, News Corp and magazines across Australia and the United Kingdom. He's worked in Moscow and Berlin – among 26 other countries – authored his first book and trained a border collie that sits before he crosses the road.

That was Lucas's first 25 years. Now he's planning to spend most of his money on booze, birds and fast cars. He read once that the rest you just squander.

ALSO IN THE SERIES

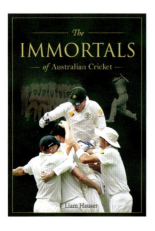

The Immortals of Australian Cricket
By Liam Hauser
ISBN: 9781925682786

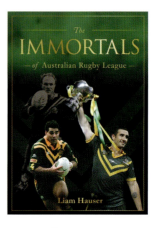

The Immortals of Australian Rugby League
By Liam Hauser
ISBN: 9781925946031

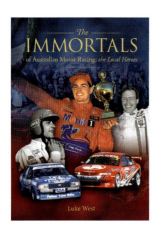

The Immortals of Australian Motor Racing: the Local Heroes
By Luke West
ISBN: 9781925946987

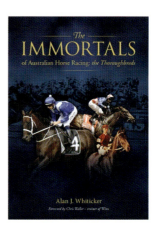

The Immortals of Australian Horse Racing: the Thoroughbreds
By Alan J. Whiticker
ISBN: 9781925946963

Available now from all good book stores.
Also visit www.geldingstreetpress.com

ARK SCHWARZER · MILE JEDINAK · C
OLAN · HARRY KEWELL · TIM CAHILL
DUKA · SAM KERR · MARK SCHWARZE
HNNY WARREN · JULIE DOLAN · HAR
RAIG JOHNSTON · MARK VIDUKA · SA
HERYL SALISBURY · JOHNNY WARREN
ISA DE VANNA · CRAIG JOHNSTON ·
ILE JEDINAK · CHERYL SALISBURY ·
WELL · TIM CAHILL · LISA DE VANNA
RR · MARK SCHWARZER · MILE JEDIN
LIE DOLAN · HARRY KEWELL · TIM C
RK VIDUKA · SAM KERR · MARK SCH
OHNNY WARREN · JULIE DOLAN · HA
AIG JOHNSTON · MARK VIDUKA · SA
HERYL SALISBURY · JOHNNY WARREN
ISA DE VANNA · CRAIG JOHNSTON ·
ILE JEDINAK · CHERYL SALISBURY ·
WELL · TIM CAHILL · LISA DE VANNA
RR · MARK SCHWARZER · MILE JEDIN
LIE DOLAN · HARRY KEWELL · TIM C
RK VIDUKA · SAM KERR · MARK SCH
OHNNY WARREN · JULIE DOLAN · HA

MARK SCHWARZER · MILE JEDINAK
DOLAN · HARRY KEWELL · TIM CAHILL
VIDUKA · SAM KERR · MARK SCHWARZER
JOHNNY WARREN · JULIE DOLAN · HA
CRAIG JOHNSTON · MARK VIDUKA · S
CHERYL SALISBURY · JOHNNY WARREN
LISA DE VANNA · CRAIG JOHNSTON
MILE JEDINAK · CHERYL SALISBURY
KEWELL · TIM CAHILL · LISA DE VANN
KERR · MARK SCHWARZER · MILE JED
JULIE DOLAN · HARRY KEWELL · TIM
MARK VIDUKA · SAM KERR · MARK SC
JOHNNY WARREN · JULIE DOLAN · H
CRAIG JOHNSTON · MARK VIDUKA · S
CHERYL SALISBURY · JOHNNY WARREN
LISA DE VANNA · CRAIG JOHNSTON
MILE JEDINAK · CHERYL SALISBURY
KEWELL · TIM CAHILL · LISA DE VANN
KERR · MARK SCHWARZER · MILE JED
JULIE DOLAN · HARRY KEWELL · TIM
MARK VIDUKA · SAM KERR · MARK SC
JOHNNY WARREN · JULIE DOLAN ·